Transactional Analysis
on the Job   Charles Albano

Communicating with Subordinates

Revised Edition / Edited by Thomasine Rendero

A Division of American Management Associations

Library of Congress Cataloging in Publication Data
Albano, Charles.
Transactional analysis on the job.

Articles reprinted from Amacom publications.
1. Psychology, Industrial—Addresses, essays, lectures. 2. Communication in management—Addresses, essays,
lectures. 3. Transactional analysis—Addresses, essays,
lectures. I. Rendero, Thomasine. II. Communicating
with subordinates. 1975. III. Title: Transactional
analysis on the job.
HF5548.8.A63   158.7   75-20236
ISBN 0-8144-5401-1

Transactional Analysis on the Job
Reprinted from *Supervisory Management*.
© 1974 AMACOM, a division of American Management Associations,
New York.

Communicating with Subordinates

© AMACOM, a division of American Management Associations, New York.
1968, 1969, 1970, 1971, 1972, 1973, 1974.

Publisher's Note

MORE AND MORE ORGANIZATIONS are beginning to realize that healthy working relationships among employees is vital for growth and success. Whether an organization is large or small, its people must communicate among themselves and with others in order to get things done. On the surface, "communicating" seems simple enough—the supervisor tells a chronically late employee that he really ought to get to work on time; the manager receives a memo from the division vice president regarding the next planning council meeting—but communication involves much more than the spoken or written word. It is a complicated process, which calls forth our past experiences and taps our senses and emotions. When someone speaks to us we do more than just translate the words into meaning. We also take in—consciously or unconsciously—the tone of voice, the raised eyebrow, the tense smile, the expression in the eyes. Usually these nonverbal messages reinforce words, but sometimes they are in conflict with them. And when the nonverbal contradicts the verbal, the results are misunderstanding, frustration, hostility.

There is proper concern among supervisors with the problems that have to do with people who interact with one another. In order to enable those whose skill in communicating plays a critical role in their efforts to maintain motivation and productivity contend with these problems, we have selected two of AMACOM's most popular reprint collections: *Transactional Analysis on the Job,* by Charles Albano, and *Communicating with Subordinates,* edited by Thomasine Rendero.

In the first part of the book, Charles Albano examines one of the most effective approaches to understanding people and what motivates their behavior: transactional analysis. In the author's view none of the many psychological concepts to which supervisors are exposed provides them with so consistent a framework for dealing with human problems peculiar to employee relations. TA's importance lies in its ability to deal with the entire range of human behavior in a consistent and understandable way. It is a tool that enables us to focus sharply on aspects of behavior that are critical in a work situation. If TA can help us understand how people relate to each other, it can help increase employee effectiveness.

The second part of the book contains selected articles from AMA-COM publications that cover both the formal and informal aspects of communication. The supervisor's success in delegating, instructing, training, counseling, criticizing, and praising relies heavily on the ability to communicate, and articles included here range from the message itself to the relationship between the people communicating.

This book, then, is addressed to supervisors at all levels of management who have the responsibility of keeping the channels of communication open and flowing among their staff. It provides a basic method for understanding the communication process between people through TA, and goes on to offer constructive ways of improving it.

Contents

Transactional Analysis on the Job
Charles Albano

How We're Programmed

Boss: "Helen, can I have the contract file for this quarter?"
Helen: "Do you want the file with the blue tab or the file with the yellow tab?"
Boss (sighing resignedly): "You know the one I need, Helen. Just give me the current file."
Helen: "Is that the one that contains the Adams letter?"
Boss (raising his eyebrows): "Well, that's a current contract item, isn't it?"
Helen: "Oh, I think I misfiled it."
Boss (completely exasperated): "Forget it! I'll find it myself. You can't do *anything* right, can you?"

This dialogue illustrates the game that transactional analysts call STUPID. Helen, who is not a new employee, initiates the game in the role of Victim. And she wins the game: She gets from her boss what she was angling for—a putdown. Another game Helen likes to play is KICK ME. The drift of this game is like that of STUPID, but the payoff is much harsher. She invariably manipulates her bosses (of which she has had quite a few) into the role of Persecutor.

This and other kinds of games (which we'll discuss more fully later on) certainly aren't in the interest of efficiency or any other company goal. What's more, they're a drain on the emotional energy of the people locked into them. So why do people play such self-defeating games?

3

Many psychologists and laymen alike see promising answers to this question in transactional analysis (TA), an approach to analyzing human behavior—in particular, the "transactions" that people make when they communicate with each other. TA was originated by Dr. Eric Berne, a clinical psychiatrist whose best-selling book, *Games People Play,* did a lot to popularize TA and generate widespread interest in his other books. The literature in the field is large and growing (see the list of references on page 54).

This article is the first in a series designed to:

1. Get across TA concepts that have management applications.
2. Illustrate these concepts by presenting and analyzing on-the-job transactions.
3. Link TA concepts to other behavioral concepts with which managers may already be familiar.

The concepts of TA and the language used to express them are simple. But they offer an impressive payoff: a way of understanding and exerting some control over your on-the-job behavior and that of others. With the insight provided by TA, you can, for example, avoid getting "hooked" into playing someone else's unproductive game. In fact, you may be able to stop the game and turn it into a straightforward transaction. You can also draw upon TA techniques to figure out:

What prompts one subordinate to put another down "without cause."

Why a fellow supervisor seems to behave naturally one moment and childishly the next.

Why and how employees store up emotions that sap their vitality at work.

Why your boss mistakenly takes offense at innocent remarks.

Why, after talking to your boss's boss, you feel as though you've been talking to the top of an iceberg.

Why you can't always find a rational explanation for an employee's behavior.

Why some very talented people seem to go out of their way to display self-defeating behavior.

Why some employees overreact to incidents of little significance.

Why you find it difficult to think "straight" under stress.

Why you are easily offended by some bosses and attracted to others.

Why your thoughts are sometimes so different from your feelings.
Why some people can't or won't accept sound advice.
Why the same activity that appeals to some workers repels others.
Why some employees repeatedly do things that bring the ceiling down on them.
Why it is that one part of you says "go" on a project and another says "no."

Stroking

Basic to an understanding of the "transactions" people make when they communicate is the principle of stroking. In playing the game of STUPID described at the beginning of this article, Helen was looking for and got what transactional analysts call a *discount*—which is a negative form of stroking. Stroking is something we all must have, whether it's negative or positive. As infants and children, most of us *literally* received positive strokes—hugs, caresses, kisses—that made us feel good. Sometimes, however, we received negative strokes in the form of physical punishment or scoldings—and bad as they made us feel, they were preferable to no strokes at all. Studies have revealed, in fact, that children who receive only negative strokes or discounts will fare infinitely better than those who receive no strokes at all. It is even possible for infants to die in the total absence of stroking.

In later life, we continue to seek "stroking" in such forms of recognition as a greeting, a compliment on appearance, praise for performance. However, we may go after discounts if no other form of stroking is available or if we have become confirmed discount-seekers.

Everyone has experienced the pain or discomfort of discounts. A manager is discounted when his boss makes a habit of going around him to communicate directly with employees. You may experience a discount when you are neither consulted about nor invited to attend a meeting on matters for which you are responsible. You are discounted when impractical goals are established without your participation and then foisted upon you for implementation. You are discounted when you are not given courtesy copies of correspondence that you feel you should have. There are many, many ways of giving people discounts, and most can easily be avoided.

The "climate" of a department or organization can be assessed by determining the stroking behavior of those in key positions and then correlating it with morale at working levels. Stroking patterns have a great deal to do with how we feel about going to work and about working once we get there.

A word of praise from a valued person at a "teachable moment" can spur an employee on to long-lasting efforts. Similarly, a single sharp discount at such a time can make it difficult for him to learn and perform well. Consider the effect of the following supervisor-to-employee discounts:

"You're not half the engineer that Ralph is."

"I'm not interested in your opinions."

"When I was your age, I had twice your experience."

The kinds of strokes we give and the kinds we seek have a telling impact on the kinds of transactions we make, the kinds of games we play. Before getting into these and other aspects of transactional analysis, however, let's take a look at the ego states that make it possible to analyze behavior.

Ego states

According to transactional analysts, every personality has three sets of programming, or ego states: Parent, Adult, and Child. (They are capitalized to differentiate them from their literal counterparts.) Individual behavior during transactions with another person is determined by the particular ego state in action at the time; the one that's activated depends on many factors—including early life experiences, the circumstances of the transaction, and the other person's ego state.

A person's behavior may stem most frequently from the same ego state—which is why we are often able to see typical or recurrent patterns of behavior. In a well-adjusted person, however, all three ego states function, with none substantially eclipsed by another. When we use them in a way appropriate to the reality of a situation, we are functioning most successfully.

Where do these ego states come from? How can we recognize them—in ourselves and in others? Let's start with the Parent ego state.

The Parent ego state

The Parent is the part of the personality containing all the instructions and guidance—the *should's, ought's, do's* and *don'ts*—that we ac-

EGO-STATE CONTRIBUTIONS TO BEHAVIOR

WHAT THE PARENT DOES	WHAT THE ADULT DOES	WHAT THE CHILD DOES
Nurtures	Processes information	Invents
Criticizes	Takes objective action	Expresses curiosity
	Thinks, then acts	
Restricts	Organizes	Acts on impulse
Judges	Plans	Acts selfishly
Blames	Solves problems	Loves
Encourages	Estimates risks	Imagines/brainstorms
Supports .	Ferrets out assumptions	Acts belligerently
		Complains
Source—the relationship between you and your parents.	*Source*—the emergence of independent thinking in early life and its subsequent development.	*Source*—the best and worst of your young self.

quire through intimate association with our parents and other authority figures in our youth. The Parent ego state (like the other two) results from a learning process. In a vast mental file cabinet of recordings, we have stored an assortment of Parent rules for living; we draw upon and use them as occasions require.

From the TA standpoint, the personality is pretty well established by the time we are six to eight years old. This early schooling came from observing our parents relate to each other and interact with others. We listened, we watched, we drew lessons. The experience was both impressive and lasting. Our feelings, too, were "recorded" and filed away. It may be difficult to reconstruct a precise impression today of any of the myriad past events in our lives. We may not even be conscious of the existence of a great number of these recordings. But psychologists and, more recently, medical researchers assure us that these recordings are "live." They do influence the way we behave today.

The Parent ego state has two sides. Various transactional analysts have referred to them as the Nurturing Parent on the one hand, and the Critical or Prejudicial Parent on the other, to reflect the opposite ways in which parents behave toward children. That is, most parents not only shelter and help their children meet the physical and emotional needs of development (nurturing behavior)—they also punish their children, if only by restricting their activities (critical behavior).

As adults, therefore, we harbor both Nurturing Parent and Critical Parent impressions. We generally draw upon them in raising a family and, significantly, in supervising subordinates. The influence of these recordings or tapes is reflected when we "come on Parent" in our dealings with others. Whether a particular response is beneficial or detrimental depends on how well suited it is to the occasion. Behavior copied and transposed intact from our parents to a current situation can

---

INDICATORS OF EGO STATES

	BODY LANGUAGE	EXPRESSIONS	VOCAL TONE
PARENT INDICATORS	Looking down over rim of glasses. Pointing an accusing finger. Hands on hip, the head leaning or straining forward. Patting on the back.	"You should . . . you ought . . . you must" "Why don't you . . ." "Stay loose" "Be cool" "Don't tell me . . ." "You disappoint me" "You always . . ." "Poor thing" "I'll protect you"	Harsh Judgmental Soothing Indignant Commanding Comforting
ADULT INDICATORS	A straight, relaxed stance. Slightly tilted head. Appearance of active listening. Regular eye contact. Confident appearance.	The offer of alternatives and options. Use of the 5 W's in questioning. "Aha, I see" "I see your point" "I recognize . . ." "How do you feel about . . ."	Relaxed Assertive Somewhat deliberative Self-assertive
CHILD INDICATORS	Forlorn appearance. Drooping shoulders. Withdrawal. Pursed lips. Scowling. Skipping. Hugging. Twinkle in eyes.	"I want" "I wish" "Wow" "I should" "If only" "Did I do okay?" "One of these days" "It's not fair" "It's not my fault" "Oh boy!"	Appealing Complaining Nagging Indignant Cheerful Protesting Grumbling Mumbling Sullen

---

arouse hostility. Our Critical Parent, for example, may unexpectedly assault a subordinate's Child ego state. When we impulsively allow the Parent to assert itself before estimating the consequences, we may well regret having done so later on.

Once we know the nature and sources of our behavior, we can more easily adopt appropriate behavior and avoid inappropriate behavior. We can't change our pasts, but it certainly helps to take the past into account. The behavior we were taught may have become outdated or inappropriate for some other reason. Recent and current social changes mandate a careful look at Parent tapes. Consider, for example, how much prevailing views have changed concerning the value of work, the role of women, the rights of management, the responsibility of employees, and many other basic values. We must be sensitive to these changes and keep an open mind toward them and their implications. Knowing our Parent will help in this and will facilitate our ability to make necessary adjustments.

On the other hand, much Parent programming is valuable. Useful habits mastered under parental guidance can carry you when the going gets rough. Habits and automatic responses based on Parent tapes can streamline efforts to make minor decisions that might otherwise consume time and effort better spent on the things that count. Consulting the Parent before making an important decision can yield worthwhile guidance; in any event, being aware of its feelings about a particular matter is important whether the advice is taken or not. Why? Because this awareness reduces internal conflict between your Parent and your Child ego states. With awareness, you conserve energy that might be wasted on an undefined, unresolved conflict—a conflict that might, in fact, keep you from making a decision.

The Adult ego state

The Adult is the problem solver. Rational and objective, it provides clear thinking and analysis—fundamental skills in managing people and situations. A manager calls upon his Adult to stand apart for an objective consideration of Parent and Child feelings, attitudes, possible prejudices. It can help gather facts, separate them from opinion and inference, analyze them, compute the effects of alternatives, and select the best one. You can make your Adult more effective by continually examining your experiences and drawing lessons from them.

Training courses in personnel management and human relations confront the manager in ways that cause him to do just that.

The Child ego state

Transactional analysts consider the Child ego state to be the most creative part of a personality. Behavior activated by the Child should be referred to as childlike, not childish. Childishness denotes immaturity—not the case in much Child-originated behavior. Like the Parent, however, the Child does initiate less desirable behavior.

The Child ego state has three parts: the Natural Child, the Manipulator, and the Adapted Child. The Natural Child is distinguished by its enjoyment of life, its need for affection, and its curiosity. The intense curiosity that the infant expresses by touching, pushing, and gripping everything in its range shows up later in laboratories, machine shops, and advertising agencies. When we don't lose too much curiosity in the process of growing up, it can spark outstanding performance, achievement, and discovery.

Our Natural Child also lets us act freely and openly with others. Transactions during this state can create feelings of warmth, friendliness, and acceptance—feelings that will satisfy our continuing need for affection. Playful, joking activity stems from the Natural Child. Creative people often describe creativity as a playful process, a toying with ideas, an urge to tinker with things and see what comes of it. Like humor, an exciting creation can result from putting things together that logically ''don't belong together.''

The Manipulator in the Child uses its potent, intuitive understanding of people to get its own sweet way. It is astute at gauging the limits of other people's endurance or tolerance. A master strategist, it can trick or con people into doing what it wants them to. We will examine its bargaining and game-playing prowess later. The Manipulator doesn't sound very constructive so far, but it can be. In toying intuitively with ideas and relationships, it can trigger inspiration, creation, and insight.

The Adapted Child results from the changes in our social behavior that we made as we grew up in order to be accepted by those around us. The roots of such behavior lie in past modes of conformity, obedience to authority, and the need to please others. A certain degree of conformity and adjustment is fine—but an overly adapted Child may

YOUR ADULT CAN HELP YOU ON THE JOB

Eric Berne has commented that the Adult performs executive functions. Before it can do so efficiently, however, it must moderate the confusion that results from conflict between Parent and Child—confusion that can keep us from attaining objectives in our best interest.

The following examples show the reaction of each ego state when the person involved is confronted with an on-the-job dilemma:

Joan is being considered for promotion to a supervisory position:

(P) "Women shouldn't be put in positions supervising men."

(A) "I can do this job and earn their allegiance. I accept the challenge."

(C) "These men won't like me if I'm promoted—but I want the job!"

Joan's Adult is well informed. It allows her the freedom she needs in order to be decisive.

George wants to delegate some of his workload—a difficult management function for many supervisors:

(P) "People are lazy. You can't turn your back on them."

(A) "Sam is competent. I've coached him and given him authority to act in my name."

(C) "If he fouls this up, I'm in trouble."

George's Adult recognized a subordinate's competence and set up conditions favorable to effective performance. A good delegator has a confident and skillful Adult.

---

hold us back today by keeping us from having full confidence in ourselves. When this happens, we fail to step out boldly in pursuit of our own inner needs and wants. An employee or a supervisor with an overadapted Child is afraid to try his wings and may fail unless he receives a lot of assurance from those around him. He needs encouragement to take more initiative and he needs reassurance that failure is a legitimate part of learning. A very dependent person may literally have to be given permission to do his own thinking.

Ways to pinpoint ego states

You can pinpoint ego states if you know what to look for. Analyze posture, facial expression, and tone of voice as well as behavior—all four are important clues to the particular ego state in action. See page 8 for a categorization of such clues by ego state.

Although it is sometimes impossible to be absolutely sure in labeling an ego state, in many cases the origins of remarks are fairly clear. Consider the following remarks made in a shop during an on-the-job training program:

"Don't weaken. I know you can succeed with a little more effort." (*Nurturing Parent*)

"Do I really have to take your hand and walk you through this simple procedure?" (*Critical Parent*)

"I'll never get the hang of this." (*Child*)

"If I learn the theory, the practice will be easy." (*Adult*)

Contaminated thinking

Sometimes Parent opinions, attitudes, and thoughts appear to us to be genuine expressions of our own objective thinking. We may express them automatically and comfortably. But when someone challenges them, we really can't defend them properly; we realize that we have never given them much thought. This is the result when the Parent contaminates the Adult.

When we express Parent prejudices and opinions directly to others or base our actions on them, we may think we are acting objectively—but we are only transmitting playbacks of old recordings. Here are some remarks that reflect Parent contamination of the Adult:

"There's no way to be an individual in a large company."

"You can't depend on any woman in a position calling for cool judgment."

"The unions will drive this country to ruin."

The more the Adult can shut out automatic hand-downs from the Parent, the more independent and objective it can be.

The Child can also influence our Adult's thinking and actions by dredging up feelings tied to some past event. Child feelings can even eclipse our thinking unless we recognize them when they come into play and take measures to deal with them. The Child within us may need comfort and reassurance.

Stressful situations heighten the danger of contamination. The fears of the Child in a person at the site of a burning house, for example, may immobilize his Adult and keep him from taking appropriate action. The same thing may happen during a hastily convened staff conference to deal with the latest "fire." Contaminated thinking usually leads to the wrong decision.

Rooted as they are in the past, contaminated thinking and behavior are often inappropriate guides to current action. Supervisors must be particularly careful to avoid such contamination because they make decisions that affect others. They *must* make every effort to be fair and impartial.

Hidden Levels of Communication

PEOPLE COMMUNICATE with each other not only to exchange information, but also to reinforce their feelings about themselves and each other. It is at this "feeling" level of communication that they make "transactions" with each other when they communicate. Such transactions on the job are very important. On the one hand, transactions can make people comfortable and free them to work productively; on the other, they can make people uncomfortable and tie up their energy in emotional conflict that renders them almost incapable of working.

The kind of transaction that two people make with each other springs from the particular combination of their respective ego states in action when they communicate. There are three basic kinds of transactions—complementary, crossed, and ulterior.

Complementary transactions

A complementary transaction is one in which the originator gets the kind of response he expects. Let's look at a sample complementary transaction between two supervisors communicating from their Adult ego states:

Henry: "How do you think the merger will affect us?"
Carl: "I think it's too soon to tell."

14

Henry's remark came from his Adult and sought an Adult response from Carl—which he got. The transaction is thus complementary, and communication is open. Both remarks deal with reality in an objective way.

Consider the following complementary Parent-Parent transaction between supervisors:

Frank: "Those new management trainees think they know it all."
Bill: "Yeah, they're all the same."

The two supervisors, operating from the Critical Parent ego state, are enjoying a good feeling because their Parents have reinforced each other on a shared attitude that they haven't stopped to evaluate. Obviously, the complementary transaction is the one used in giving positive strokes.

Here's a complementary Child-Parent transaction between a harried salesman and his boss:

Lou: "I've got to have some help selling Mac—that tough old bird at the Lakeland account. He stops me cold no matter what I do. Can you help?"
Boss: "Sure, sure. Don't worry about it. I'll go see him."

In this complementary transaction, Lou's Child "hooked" his boss's Nurturing Parent, and Lou got the support he wanted. This kind of support, certainly in large doses, will make Lou dependent.

The next type of transaction, the crossed transaction, occurs when a gambit from one person's ego state draws forth a quite different response from the one expected. As we will see, this tends to stop communication.

Crossed transactions

Let's go back to the merger discussion between supervisors Henry and Carl to show how a different response from Carl can result in a crossed rather than a complementary transaction:

Henry: "How do you think the merger will affect us?"
Carl: "You'd be better off concentrating on your department instead

of worrying about the merger. You can't afford to waste any time.''

Here, Henry's Adult request for information failed to draw forth an Adult response. Instead, it met with a discount from Carl's Critical Parent. Putdowns like this are all too common on the job—not only because of the competitive spirit in many organizations, but also because our educational system stresses the ability to be critical and evaluative. When we use our highly developed critical faculties inappropriately, we discount other people—making them feel bad. Because crossed transactions can wound people, they can stop or restrict communication and they can destroy the cooperative relations necessary to effective organization functioning.

Let's turn the complementary transaction between salesman Lou and his boss into a crossed one:

Lou: "I've got to have some help selling Mac—that tough old bird at the Lakeland account. He stops me cold no matter what I do. Can you help?"

Boss: "Why does everybody come crying to me with their problems? I have more than enough to do as it is!''

Instead of the expected Parent response, Lou's Child gets a response from his boss's Child. Both men are complaining; neither is helpful. Both feel discounted.

Maintaining your Adult

If Lou's boss had been familiar with the concepts and techniques of transactional analysis, he might have suspected Lou's gambit to be an attempt to "hook" his Nurturing Parent—and he might have resisted both the hook and an impulse to respond from his Child. Let's look at the situation as Lou's boss might have altered it.

Lou: "I've got to have some help selling Mac—that tough old bird at the Lakeland account. He stops me cold no matter what I do. Can you help?"

Boss: "I think so. Tell me, when do you call on him?"

Lou: "Every Monday morning—and most of the time he won't even see me."

Boss: "It might help you to know that Mac doesn't really warm up to *anything* until after his two martinis with lunch—and on Monday, he warms up more slowly than usual. The best time to call on him is Tuesday or Wednesday afternoon around three o'clock."

What has Lou's boss done here? He has responded to Lou's Child from his Adult. In consciously choosing this course of action, he accomplished two important things: (1) He avoided putting Lou off or stepping in and taking over for him, and (2) his response kept the relationship on an objective basis and gave Lou a chance to try again, this time from his Adult. The persistent use of the Adult in such a situation encourages the other person to do likewise. When this happens, communication is open and it can be productive. Initially, of course, the transaction is crossed. Although there is a possibility that this may stop communication, it is more likely to improve communication if the Adult is used persistently.

Ulterior transactions

The third basic kind of transaction is called ulterior because it involves hidden messages between ego states that are different from the surface or apparent ones. In the following example, Sally's boss is referring to a memo that Sally has already had to retype twice:

Boss: "That's the third draft. It doesn't have to be letter-perfect."
Sally: "I'm finishing it up now."

At first glance, this would seem to be an Adult-Adult transaction. At the surfa ͜ level it is, but at the psychological level it is a Parent-Child confrontation (as Sally and her boss know very well because they know each other very well). At the hidden level, the transaction goes like this:

Boss: "I'll have to settle for your third draft even if it is messy. Your carelessness is holding everything up."
Sally: "Here's your old draft. I'm tired of being picked on for erasures and minor errors."

Too often, we find it easier to hold our feelings in rather than level with each other. But they find their tortuous way out at the hidden level. Like the crossed transaction, the ulterior transaction can also wound—and cause even greater resentment because the participants aren't being open with each other.

Angular transactions

An angular transaction is a variation of the ulterior transaction. In an angular transaction, the sender's message is deliberately expressed in a way that allows it to appeal to two ego states in the receiver. This is done to manipulate the receiver into a desired course of action. The sender can feel safe because if his attempt at manipulation backfires, he can disclaim it by saying that he was misunderstood. The angular transaction can also be used to sound people out about their feelings and intentions or to get them to say something they may later regret.

Here's an example of how a supervisor maliciously initiates an angular transaction with another supervisor: "I was certainly surprised to hear that you were passed over for promotion. What will you do now?"

Ostensibly an Adult-to-Adult gambit, this comment is designed to draw forth—if possible—a Child response such as, "I'll quit, that's what! *Then* they'll be in the soup." Timed properly, the angular transaction may succeed in eliciting such a response.

True communication is the accurate exchange of meaning and intent among people. The difficulty in achieving it lies in the fact that people hear, see, and understand according to their experiences and their expectations. Because of this, some people view almost all transactions as ulterior. At an early age, they were exposed to many ulterior transactions; their expectations for subsequent transactions were "set." For such people, the meaning of a message often lies more in them than in the sender. Their pasts have overwhelmed them; as a result, they are not reacting realistically to many situations in the present.

Life positions

The way we feel—about ourselves and others—determines to a large extent the kinds of transactions we make with other people, the kinds of strokes we give and seek, the kinds of games we play.

A FORMIDABLE INFLUENCE

Your life position has a formidable influence on your relations with other people because it preconditions every encounter you have with others. It will influence, for example, the kinds of jobs you may be successful at; the heights you may achieve; the lengths to which you may go in order *not* to achieve; the company you keep; the number and quality of friendships you enjoy—in short, the quality of your life. Can you think of anything more basic and more consequential in your life than your life position?

Basically, there are two ways we can feel about other people and ourselves—OK or Not OK. A person who feels OK about himself at heart accepts himself as good and sound. He feels that he is worthwhile as a person, so he doesn't have to spend a great deal of energy trying to demonstrate to others or to himself that he is, in fact, OK. A person feels OK or Not OK from the Child ego state. Typically, this very basic feeling is a carry-over from our formative years. The accumulation of feelings that resulted from early contacts with our parents shaped and hardened the way we think and feel toward self and others—a fundamental position transactional analysts call a *life position*. We made this weighty judgment at a time when we were, unfortunately, not up to making it. Unless we later give the matter much thought and make conscious efforts to change it—in some cases, with the help of therapeutic counseling—the position we took back then will continue to govern our actions.

Here is a list of the four life positions. It is important to recognize the implications of each if we are to account for behavior at work and master our own responses. It should be noted that although these positions operate at a largely unconscious level in maturity, they underlie all our behavior.

1. I'm OK—You're OK
2. I'm Not OK—You're OK
3. I'm Not OK—You're Not OK
4. I'm OK—You're Not OK

A person in position Number 1 (I'm OK—You're OK) is a pleasure to everyone concerned. Unlike the other three, which solidify in youth, this position (according to transactional analysts) is finally decided upon in maturity. Herein lies the hope for change through conscious effort by adults who sincerely want to change their lives. The I'm OK—You're OK person is free of the basic hang-ups that result from Not OK feelings; he does not play psychological games. He is prepared to roll up his sleeves and get on with the work. This winner's position allows him to live up to his capabilities and achieve his objectives. He does not have to squander energy on building protective façades, and he does not feel compelled to "check out" the "OK-ness" of other people.

Position Number 2 (I'm Not OK—You're OK) is a kind of servile, self-demeaning stance in relation to others. It is a loser's position; the person who holds it feels inferior and is unlikely to attain happiness even if he achieves some success. No matter what happens, it is hard for him to feel good about himself. The pleasure of a recent promotion quickly gives way to anxiety over the next. He is concerned with the approval of others and may work hard to get it. But even this does not bring lasting satisfaction or relief. Because he does not feel good about himself at heart, he finds it difficult to enjoy compliments about himself or his work. His Not OK Child fears failure or rejection and throws up its defenses.

Though he may appear at times to be unconcerned about what others think of him or his work, he really cares a great deal. He may have a tendency to withdraw from others. He needs reassurance and recognition, but most of all he needs a supervisor who demonstrates recognition of his worth as a person apart from his successes or failures. Such an employee can progress well under a supervisor whose predominant style is Nurturing Parent or Adult, but would be completely stunted under a Critical Parent style. Why? Because he would tend to accept Critical Parent rebukes as a true reflection of his personal worth. The best that he would be capable of producing would probably come from his Adapted Child. It would be uninspired, conforming, routine behavior. He would never break out of his shell.

Position Number 3 (I'm Not OK—You're Not OK) is extremely difficult to cope with because it is so negative toward self and others. The employee who holds it may distrust everyone and see little worth in life and work—certainly a loser's position. It would take an extraordinarily sensitive, patient, and understanding supervisor to get through to such a worker. In this as in the other positions there are, of course, degrees of OKness and not OKness. Extreme, absolute negativity is fortunately the exception and is treated by professional therapists. Where the position is not extreme, a supervisor can with understanding and patience overcome distrust and build confidence. Such an approach is essential in successful supervision of this kind of person. Some so-called hard-core unemployables may be in this category.

Position Number 4 (I'm OK—You're Not OK) is one in which a person feels good about himself but distrusts and may well look down on others. Such an employee tends to feel superior to others and, to the degree that he does, his supervisor will find it difficult to integrate him into the work team. Though he is likely to be pushy and offensive toward others, he will react indignantly if efforts are made to correct or change him. Since he finds others Not OK, he tends to drive people away. He also tends to come on in his Critical Parent and to offend the Child in others. Paradoxically, he plays the persecutor toward others even though he sees himself as a victim of people out to take advantage of him. However, he may come to accept others on a one-to-one basis after a trial period during which he assures himself that they are not out to ''get'' him. With such a subordinate, a supervisor must retain his composure at all times and use his Adult and Child appropriately to win the subordinate's respect and allegiance. It is helpful to engage him in Child-Child transactions of the kind that can release tension and build rapport.

The strength of the life positions probably accounts for a great deal of our difficulty in relating to others. Confronted with extreme Not OKness in a subordinate, we may give up and raise our hands in disgust. The supervisor who has his own Not OK Child to contend with is going to find it difficult to bring about change in employees in life positions Number 3 and Number 4. He will come up short in dealing with Number 3, and he will probably be the object of a good deal of persecution and game playing in situation Number 4.

Fortunately for all of us, these life positions can be reconsidered by the Adult and, with persistence, we can change. We can learn to feel good about ourselves and others and practice new, more appropriate behavior that can make us feel better.

Role playing

Depending upon our inclination to dominate or to be dominated by others, we may be masters of the art of role playing. TA identifies three basic roles—Victim, Persecutor, and Rescuer. Capitalizing these roles indicates that they are parts played in order to manipulate or take advantage of others. There are times when circumstances cast a supervisor in the role of persecutor—for example, when he must fire an employee. And there are times when economic conditions make actual victims of people during plant closedowns and staff reductions. These are distinct from Persecutors and Victims of the role-playing variety who make others suffer needlessly or who seemingly thrive on victimization.

The Rescuer feels impelled to make people dependent on him. He does this by assuming their responsibilities, handling their more difficult assignments, holding back company information they need in order to proceed confidently with their work. He strives to make sure that his people fail to develop their full potential or ever come to realize that they can be successful without him.

Psychological games

Victim, Persecutor, Rescuer—these are the starring roles in psychological game playing, an important element in the TA approach to understanding behavior. TA game theory hits home for many of us because we have on occasion played psychological games or come up against others who do—even though we may have had no labels for the games and even though we may not have been able to pinpoint precisely what was happening or what was at stake.

Like ordinary games, psychological games offer rewards that motivate players. Unlike ordinary games, most psychological ones are played unconsciously. In both instances, players pass away time, interact, and secure payoffs they value for one reason or another. But the payoff doesn't come in chips, cash, or high numerical tabulations. The payoff is in feelings. Paradoxically, in psychological games "losers" can "win" and "winners" can "lose"—since the object of many such games is to reap or give bad feelings. These games are clearly destructive of good human relations. And since more than two can play simultaneously, human costs to the organization can be staggering.

Psychological game playing requires skillful, practiced players. To play the games "successfully," people must reliably play out the steps required by their roles. If, for example, the preferred role is Victim, the player knows how to (1) catch the interest of game players who like to play Persecutor or Rescuer, (2) begin a transaction that gives another player (or other players) the opportunity to step in, and (3) know precisely when to alter his behavior in some dramatic way to make the payoff materialize. These skills are usually developed over a period of years, although some people seem to be "naturals."

The "feeling" payoffs can take many forms—anger, increased distrust, disappointment, vengeance, and a heightened sense of superiority or inferiority, to name a few. Employees may use these feelings to get sympathy from others, to hurt them further, or to close or widen the psychological distance between them. By using feelings manipulatively, the game player brings some people under his control and drives others off. A person who sets out—consciously or unconsciously—to satisfy or reinforce Not OK feelings will play games frequently. They become his constant crutch in "getting along" with others.

Games, then, are recurring patterns of behavior fueled by hidden motives. Their salient feature is that *real motives are hidden*. Neither player acknowledges them and, as noted before, neither is usually aware of his precise motives for playing. This is why they can be so devastating to us as decision makers, as people held accountable for the behavior of others.

The effects of hidden feelings

Games certainly make for dishonest relationships—involving, as they do, ulterior motives and hidden feelings. They always result in avoiding authentic contact with others. If the other person is Not OK, how can he be trusted? He can't; he must be kept in his place—at a safe distance. To accomplish this, the game player discounts (abuses, belittles) the other person. The manager who deals in discounts, or negative strokes, must live with the negative consequences that result. These are summarized in the box on page 24.

EFFECTS OF REPEATED DISCOUNTING

If the Employee's Life Position is:	Discounting May Result in:
I'm OK—You're OK	Modifying it to I'm OK— You're Not OK
I'm OK—You're Not OK	Confirming this position
I'm Not OK—You're Not OK	Confirming this position
I'm Not OK—You're OK	Modifying it to I'm Not OK —You're Not OK

Note that the "I'm OK" aspect of a life position is resistant to discounting. For the person with this basic feeling, a discounting manager is simply proving that *he's* Not OK. However, OK—Not OK positions are seldom absolute in the sense that *all* other people are seen as Not OK or that they are seen as 100 percent Not OK. OKness is a matter of degree, and we make exceptions—so another person's standing with us is subject to change, for better or worse.

In view of the effects of discounting, it is obviously wise to confine reprimands to a subordinate's undesirable *behavior* and avoid attacking him as a person. That is, instead of saying "You are this and you are that and therefore you are not acceptable to me," your approach should be "Doing this or doing that is not acceptable to me." Similarly, the old guidelines of disciplining in private and praising in public still hold water.

Even though the price tag on game-playing behavior may be very high, games go on because they are usually unconscious; they satisfy a basic need to fill time in a way that reinforces life positions, thus reassuring the player that he is "alive and well"; they bring rewards in the form of feelings that the player collects. Gamesters associate with other gamesters, of course, and many games complement each other. For example, an employee who plays STUPID, KICK ME, and other Victim-oriented games may well be found working for a supervisor who enjoys his role in such Persecutor games as NIGYSOB (to be explained later in detail).

Just as there are degrees of OKness and Not OKness, so are there degrees of acceptability among games. The games played by most people at work are mild in comparison with games involving costly payoffs—games that may end, as Eric Berne noted, in courtrooms, jail cells, and morgues.

Let's take a look at some specific games played on the job. A supervisor, like an employee, may be drawn into them without realizing it.

NIGYSOB

The game called NIGYSOB ("Now I've Got You, You S.O.B.") results in confirming the player's conviction that the respondent is unreliable. The payoff is a discount for the respondent, who typically plays such complementary games as STUPID and KICK ME.

Mark, who runs a large warehouse stocked with various home furnishings, likes to play NIGYSOB. He runs the warehouse like a martinet, setting impossible goals for his subordinates and then indulging himself in angry explosions when they fail to measure up. Mark often operates from his Critical Parent—and the subordinates who have stayed with him reciprocate with their Adapted Child. Here's a sample NIGYSOB game between Mark and his assistant:

Mark: "What's the inventory level now on Number 603 red floor tile—not counting the orders that have been received but not filled yet?"

Assistant: "Well, I don't know exactly. It's turning over fast because headquarters gave it a 15 percent discount. It's somewhere between 25 and 27 cases. I'll know more exactly when I hear from the eastern salesman. They. . . ."

Mark: "Don't give me any excuses! I want up-to-the minute inventory counts—and you know it! If you can't keep up with them, find a job that's better suited to your mentality!"

Obviously, Mark's life position is I'm OK—You're Not OK, one in which his assistant concurs. Actually, Mark's assistant could simply have replied "26 cases" to Mark's question, but that would have stopped the game short of a payoff.

When Mark fails to set up a NIGYSOB game, his assistant initiates a KICK ME game—and, of course, Mark obliges. Despite the frequency with which they play and "win," they are both losers in the long run—and the warehouse suffers, too.

BLEMISH

In the following example, a supervisor with a You're Not OK life position is out to drive his point home with an employee who doesn't concur with his boss's position toward him. The name of the game is BLEMISH.

Supervisor: "Harry, how soon can you get me a runoff of the payroll breakdown?"

Harry: "I have it here. See—it includes the latest column refinements."

Supervisor: "Wait a minute. What's that?"

Harry: "Just a spacing error."

Supervisor: "Just a spacing error! This is intolerable!"

Harry: "But it doesn't change the report in any way."

Supervisor: "That doesn't matter. You ought to know better than to try to get away with slipshod work like this."

This is a game the boss always "wins." If the subordinate strenuously objects, the boss could persecute him more vigorously and escalate the situation into a game called UPROAR. Then they would trade abuses that would lead to extreme behavior. Someone might throw a punch. Someone might be fired. Even if the payoff isn't final, each can take pleasure in knowing that he was absolutely right in what he did. Why, he must have had the other person pegged right from the very start.

YES, BUT

A popular game around the office is YES, BUT. It may be played as follows:

Carol: "I'd like you to do an article on training for the company newsletter."

George: "I wish I could help you, but I'm awfully busy on this project."

Carol: "Mr. Farrell told me you could put it aside."

George: "Yes, but if I did that I'd never meet the deadline."

Carol: "I'll get some temporary help for you."

George: "The last thing I need is those dumb temporary people who don't know which end is up."

Carol: "You can show them how you want things done."

George: "Yes, but if I do that I won't have any time to do your article."

As you can see, the game can be carried on to impressive heights of absurdity. Although the voiced level of communication is mostly on an Adult-Adult basis, at the hidden level a Parent-Child transaction is in progress. Carol is coming on Parent, trying to give instruction and help to George's stubborn Child. George's Child is replying, in effect, "Nothing you say is going to influence me." It takes considerable skill to contend with master game players who have refined their craft through long practice.

A related game is WHY DON'T YOU . . . YES, BUT. In it, the hidden Parent-Child transactions are more evident. Supervisors and others who have a tendency to advise people or play Rescuer find themselves on the WHY DON'T YOU end of the game. Here's a sample game in progress:

Supervisor: "How are you doing at night school?"

Employee: "Not well; it's too time consuming."

Supervisor: "Why don't you take fewer courses?"

Employee: "Yes, I could do that—but it would take so much longer to complete the program."

Supervisor: "Why don't you reduce the course load by spreading it out? You could attend during the summer."

Employee: "Yes, but if I did that I wouldn't have time for my family."

Supervisor: "Well, you could arrange your courses during the school year so that you attend only one night per week."

Employee: "Yes, but that would mean using up my electives in taking courses that I don't want."

Supervisor: "Why don't you. . . ."

The game goes on and on nonproductively, with each player trying to best the other, as in a contest of wits. Playing such games is not only an insecure way for people to relate to each other, but it can also be extremely time consuming and costly to management.

Another on-the-job game is the AIN'T IT AWFUL game. Like other games, this one is nonproductive—even though positive stroking rather than discounting is involved. In the following example, Hank is playing AIN'T IT AWFUL with a fellow supervisor who is in the habit of playing it with him.

Hank: "You try to do a job around here and what do you get?"
Fellow supervisor: "I know what you mean; it's awful."
Hank: "I don't know why I put up with it."
Fellow supervisor: "They're incapable of appreciating good work and dedication."
Hank: "You'd think they'd change their ways before it's too late."
Fellow supervisor: "They wouldn't know how to."

Does this dialogue resolve or change anything? No. Despite the shared joy of a mutual Parent attitude, Hank does not learn from his experience, and his companion has not shed light on anything.

AIN'T IT AWFUL lends itself to team operations. Too often, task forces or committees authorized to study problems and make recommendations for action forsake analysis of the problems in favor of going on a Parent-Parent binge. Much time is spent expressing concern, regret, and disgust—but nothing is done. The members never come to grips with root problems. Their collective Adult waits its turn while the Parents play their game. An infrequency and low-level intensity of game playing certainly are good indications of an organization's health.

Understanding games and their effects

To understand game playing, the supervisor must (1) note the kinds of feelings collected as payoffs and (2) watch the frequency with which players play. Once a supervisor identifies games, he can begin to reduce their frequency and intensity. A good place to begin is with one's own behavior. The questions to ask here are: "Am I easily hooked into other people's games? Do I repeatedly do things that bring on bad feelings? Do I insist upon advising or rebuking people even when no good will come of it? Do I seize every opportunity to get back at 'offenders'?" A supervisor must use his Adult to mediate his actions in such matters. If he does not, he is likely to become hunter or prey in unceasing games.

HOW LIFE POSITION INFLUENCES EMPLOYEE BEHAVIOR

AN EMPLOYEE— ...When His Life Position Is:	Communicates	Accepts Delegation	Develops	Handles Disagreement	Solves Problems	Spends Time	Is Moved to Act	Feels Toward Others
I'M OK – YOU'RE OK	Openly	Readily	Independently, Learns Willingly	By Seeking Clarification and Mutual Resolution	By Consulting Others, Trusting Himself	Taking Necessary Action and Producing	On Assignment or Initiative	Equal
I'M NOT OK – YOU'RE OK	Defensively Self-Deprecatingly	Timidly	Slowly; Needs Reassurance and Coaching	By Perceiving Differences in Opinion as Evidence of His Inadequacy	By Relying Almost Completely on Others	Brooding or Overcompensating in Constant Activity	By Praise or Admonition	Inferior
I'M OK – YOU'RE NOT OK	Defensively Aggressively	By Procrastinating, Bickering, and Bargaining	With Difficulty; Learning Is Blocked	By Placing Blame on Others	By Unilaterally Rejecting Others' Ideas	Boasting, Provoking Others, Playing Persecutor	When Forced; May Demand Official Instructions	Superior
I'M NOT OK – YOU'RE NOT OK	Hostilely Abruptly	By Trying to Beg Off, Delegating Upward. Unwillingly Accepts Responsibility	With Difficulty; Withdraws and Repeats Errors	By Escalating the Conflict; Involving a Third Party	By Succumbing to Problems	Withdrawing; Playing a Variety of Games	By Reprimands or Threats	Despondent Alienated

How do people who work for a game-playing supervisor behave? Usually, they respond either by learning to play the games involved, or by withdrawing and becoming passive. In an effort to protect themselves from persecution that they don't understand and can't attribute to their own behavior, subordinates usually resort to defensive reporting. An employee who feels victimized may decide that the safest route to survival is to:

- Tell the boss what he wants to hear, even if it's a lie.
- Tell him no more than what he specifically asks for.
- Tell him nothing that can lead to punishment.

The supervisor whose behavior triggers these reactions is self-defeating, because timely, accurate, complete information is the life-blood of organizations. Moreover, such supervisory behavior exemplifies the phenomenon called the "self-fulfilling prophecy": The supervisor involved acts in a way that brings forth undesirable behavior he had predicted in his subordinates at the outset. In other words, treat a subordinate as though he can't be trusted, and soon he will become untrustworthy. Treat him as though he has no initiative, and he will fulfill your expectation.

How games are halted: It takes two to play

Since games are played to obtain payoffs, the best thing a supervisor can do to stop one is to withhold the payoff. Half a transaction does not make a game. If an employee is playing KICK ME, don't kick him. That just reinforces his behavior. Instead, use your Adult in calling upon him to use his Adult to change his behavior. Persistence in using your Adult can get him to recognize the deficiency of his behavior and commit himself to changing it.

Don't, however, tell him that you think he is playing a psychological game. He may not understand and will resent your psychologizing. Even if he does understand, he's not likely to admit to anything. Disclosure may even strengthen his resolve to play games. If you lose your perspective and come on with your Critical Parent, you provide the expected payoff and continue the game. If the game is STUPID, refuse to imply that you think him stupid. You can expect a tough struggle with your own Critical Parent in this—but you must center on the *behavior* of the person, not his personal attributes, whatever they may be.

When you separate the person from the act, his Not OK feelings will diminish because you are neither reinforcing nor threatening his self-concept. Your relationship will be one in which you can respect and stroke the person and continue to expect behavioral change for the better. Games can be ended only by an Adult determination to find other, more genuine ways to get along. In the same manner, life positions can be changed to I'm OK—You're OK. These changes do not come easily. They have to be worked at in an environment that makes it possible for people to grow and develop.

Styles of supervision

LEADERSHIP STYLES have been characterized by the use of numbered grids, behavior scales or continuums, and such various terms as autocrat, benevolent autocrat, joiner, quarterback, seller, and bureaucrat. Describing them in TA terms can shed some light on the way we use our ego states in leadership situations. Where a style is not working for a supervisor because his predominant ego state tends to put people off or put them down, he can change it by appropriately using other ego states more often. A knowledge of TA style possibilities makes change easier. The only caution here is that in using behavior from other ego states, the supervisor must be sincere. To be otherwise would be manipulative. It would be "playing a role"—and, in the end, he would find himself less effective than before.

Style, for our purposes, is "the way a supervisor relates to his employees in getting a job done and in meeting overall objectives." A supervisor's style shows in how he gets others to perform, how he gets along with others, and how he interprets his responsibilities. Style change should be undertaken only after a careful analysis of the ways in which he relates to others and the ways in which others expect him to behave. The nature of the work being performed, of course, should also be taken into account. The idea is to become aware of the style he is using and the impact of that style on the effective management of others. Take a look at the following style classifications, which are based on the use of a predominant ego state.

The Natural Child supervisor

The Natural Child supervisor too often uses the inappropriate and least admirable traits of the Child ego state. He is selfish, and he is not committed to furthering the goals either of subordinates or of the organization. His behavior ranges from being chummy with subordinates to withdrawal and passivity to occasional outbursts or temper tantrums when he is criticized for not performing. Although he easily makes friends with one or two subordinates (by appealing to their Child), he blatantly plays favorites and stirs up resentment in doing so. Moreover, he can with equal ease alienate the one or two friends he does make. He does not recognize or admit that he is particularly ineffective and usually responds to such charges by pointing out behavior in colleagues that he feels is going unnoticed by higher management. He claims that he is being singled out for critical treatment—and he makes this feeling known even to those who work for him. As a result, his subordinates lose respect for him and the organization; they may take advantage of a situation in which they are not required to produce.

This kind of supervisor is obviously not effective as a leader. Good performers leave him at the first opportunity. Ineffective subordinates remain with him or gravitate toward him—giving his department a reputation for being a kind of limbo for people in transit or on their way out. Important work is shifted from him to other supervisors—who often resent having to accommodate it. They feel that they are being burdened because of higher management's unwillingness to confront him with his shortcomings. Such a supervisor saps the vitality of the organization in several ways. First, because others have to salvage work that he began, he is responsible for a situation in which nonperformance is rewarded and performance is punished. The other supervisors who do the salvage work resent this situation. And the same resentment permeates working levels, where it is expressed in discontent with which other supervisors must deal.

No positive strokes come from this supervisor. He tends to use crooked and very conditional strokes in his dealings with others. He puts across the message, "I'll like you *if . . .*" (you do things exactly my way, you make me look good to my boss, you cater to my personal whims, etc.). His games, which are an important part of his existence, tend to be of the "If it weren't for (you)" variety. Employees seeking guidance or coaching from him generally find themselves in crossed transactions. They address him on an Adult-to-Adult basis, but he responds irresponsibly from his Child.

Further characteristics—This supervisor tends to maintain an I'm Not OK—You're Not OK life position. He is variously aloof, frenetically playful, indecisive, unconcerned, uncommitted, whining, selfish, and complaining. Making a decision is anathema to him. Just as his favorite role is Victim, his favorite associates are other Victims and Rescuers. Motto: "Why don't they get off my back?" Games played: WHY DOES THIS ALWAYS HAPPEN TO ME? KICK ME, STUPID, AIN'T IT AWFUL, IF IT WEREN'T FOR. . . .

The Critical Parent supervisor

The Critical Parent supervisor wants and insists upon maximum production, but seldom gets it. Although his chief means of communicating with others is Critical Parent to Child, he may use Nurturing Parent behavior in a last-ditch attempt at manipulation. People see through him easily, and they resent being treated as children who can't be trusted to be responsible for their own behavior. Using threats and intimidation to get his way, he frequently puts people down and seldom can bring himself to give praise or other rewards for performance. He resents being so seldom stroked himself, and seems to operate on the assumption that he and everyone else must constantly prove themselves acceptable as human beings. Any positive stroking on his part is brief, very conditional (given only when his exacting standards are met), and frequently diluted: "Not a bad job, considering. . . ."

His subordinates feel that no matter what they do, no matter how hard they work, there is no pleasing him. His behavior fosters emotional and intellectual dependency—with the result that people find it difficult to grow and develop under him. His style attracts people with Not OK Child feelings to work for him. He creates an atmosphere in which they can play games that confirm their Not OK feelings.

Further characteristics—This supervisor handles conflict by oppressive means; the direction of his communication is primarily downward and one-way. His favorite role is Persecutor, which fits his I'm OK—You're Not OK life position. Motto: "I'll do the thinking. You do what you're told.'' Games played: BLEMISH, CORNER, NOW I'VE GOT YOU, YOU S.O.B.

The Nurturing Parent supervisor

The Nurturing Parent supervisor strokes people unconditionally for being people—because he likes them and wants to be liked in return. The trouble is that he tolerates minimal performance and usually pitches in to help the work along. Self-motivated achievers may fare well with him if they themselves provide the initiative necessary to forge ahead—to grow personally and professionally on the job. Things tend to remain static in his department even though morale for most people in his rather close work group is high. If the supervisor is a true rescuer, people can and will develop in his organization. After all, he does value such development, and he knows it doesn't happen accidentally. But his subordinates will develop slowly in a minimum-risk, low-key atmosphere.

If he's a role-playing Rescuer, it's important for him to maintain their dependence upon him. He may even set people up to fail and afterward lull them into continued dependence. He will play games to the extent necessary to achieve these results. Whenever possible, he will create an image for subordinates that he alone stands between them and a hard-crusted, insensitive management. This is to ensure that they will value him all the more.

Further characteristics—This supervisor tends to have an I'm OK—You're Not OK life position, and the primary direction of his communication is downward. The honest rescuer type of Nurturing Parent has this motto: "Don't worry about things. We'll work them out." The manipulatory Rescuer takes a different tack: "What would you do without me?" Games played include I'M ONLY TRYING TO HELP YOU and LET'S YOU AND HIM FIGHT.

The Adapted Child supervisor

The chief concern of the Adapted Child supervisor is to perform precisely to the minimal degree necessary. A foot-dragger who has to be badgered into better performance, he seeks acceptance from everyone. As a result, he hesitates to go out or to innovate. He exercises great skill to avoid offending anyone and may use his Manipulative Child to assure his aims. Because he has trouble unleashing his Natural Child, he lacks creativity and joy in achievement.

This supervisor is the product of organizations or supervisors who discount innovative, aggressive behavior. Over a period of time, he has developed a compulsion to secure his status through carefully prescribed behavior. He tends to be conservative, accepting of others, and upward-oriented in his needs for dependency. Faced with a decision that he feels may be unpopular, he will try to delegate it upward. If this fails, he will probably procrastinate, hoping that the problem will go away if he waits it out. He has a tendency to be apologetic and defensive. When things get tough, he starts buck-passing and fault-finding.

Further characteristics—The primary direction of this supervisor's communication is upward. Because he is heavily dependent for his inner security upon authority figures and their estimate of his work (and worth), he tends to behave as though he has an "I'm OK *if*— You're OK *if* . . . life position. At all costs he will avoid organizational and interpersonal conflict. Games played: SEE WHAT YOU MADE ME DO, IF IT WEREN'T FOR. . . .

The Adult supervisor

The Adult supervisor is not one who always acts from his Adult ego state. Rather, he uses his Adult to filter and assemble his thoughts before he acts. Then, when he does act, it's in a way appropriate to the needs of the situation. He may act from any of his ego states, but he will do so only after consulting his Adult. He can supervise a broad range of employees effectively. He is as much concerned about them as persons as he is with getting a job done well.

Because this supervisor can communicate with people on a variety of levels, he is a good motivator and team builder; he can deal well with individuals or groups. He knows when to joke and how to em-phathize with others, and he finds it easy to be candid with people. When rewards are in order, he has no difficulty in stroking subordinates. People like him because he is capable of accepting them as they are while urging them on to further growth and development. He does not play roles. He does not "put on." He levels with his people and asks that they do so with him. People feel free to approach him because they know from experience that he will not put them down or put them off.

He does not foster dependency, but encourages people to deal with problems from their Adult. He is a good delegator, a supervisor who expects each person to perform to the degree to which he is capable. His is possibly the only style of supervision in which deliberately straight strokes (good feelings, rewards) are commonly and honestly given.

Further characteristics—Such a supervisor has an I'm OK—You're OK life position. His motto: "Together, we can do almost anything." He does not manipulate others, and he does not play games.

The supervisory styles described above are not likely to exist in such extreme, pure states. Like everyone, supervisors have three ego states; their behavior should shift from one state to another according to the demands of the situation and their best interpretation of what is appropriate behavior for effective supervision under the circumstances. However, taking a look at these styles in their pure states should make it easier for a supervisor to understand the sources of his behavior.

Many supervisors have a favorite or habitual style based primarily on use of one or two of the styles discussed. A style is good to the degree that it lends itself to the accomplishment of objectives and produces satisfying human relations. If either is lacking, some change is in order. Change can start with more concern for people or more concern for getting work done, or both.

A supervisor who habitually uses the Critical Parent to meet objectives does so at a high cost to the people who work for him—and to the productivity of his department. Change for him will mean more trusting, more nurturing behavior toward others. He will have to delegate more fully and reward performance if he is to be more effective. His supervisory practices will have to aim at developing rather than at discounting people. If he recognizes himself as a psychological game player, he will need to stop his games and learn to derive satisfaction from authentic, straightforward transactions. When he learns to stroke employees as people as well as for what they do, he will be well on the way to improving his effectiveness.

There is no ideal supervisory profile—though some are obviously better than others. Neither is there one "real" ego state. All of them are "real" in the sense that they are different presentations appropriate to different environments. Most people can and do alter their behavior in different circumstances. Some people, however, do not. Their rigid behavior stems from their almost exclusive use of Parent, Adult, or Child. On a day-to-day basis in a single setting—such as work—supervisors do tend to present themselves in a habitual way. This is why there is value in studying styles. When a supervisor's style becomes rigid, his effectiveness diminishes.

Motivation and Counseling

MOTIVATION AND COUNSELING are two of the best methods a super-visor has for raising employee productivity and performance levels. Let's take a look first at motivation and then at counseling to see the ways in which TA techniques can increase the effectiveness with which a supervisor uses these methods.

Motivation in the TA sense requires consideration of each ego state to encourage a worker to reach departmental goals. The highest level of motivation flourishes in a job where he or she can get strokes for all three ego states. Remember that a worker who is unable to find satis-factory positive strokes from the job for his Parent, Adult, and Child won't hesitate to disrupt work to get any kind of strokes at all from you or from his co-workers.

He may, for example, play KICK ME with you, BLEMISH with a younger worker, or AIN'T IT AWFUL with a peer. All stroke searches of this nature are counterproductive. Whether a worker goes after a put-down from you or indulges in Parent-Parent binges with his peers, he wastes hours of his own and others' time.

But, you may say, do I really have to pay attention to the Parent, Adult, and Child of every subordinate? That triples my staff! The an-swer is *yes*—do so selectively and appropriately, and you will also increase efficiency or output. Take the Parent ego state, for example. Parent tapes contain many, many messages concerning what work we do, what satisfaction it gives, what values should be placed on various kinds of work, what constitutes fair treatment at work, what obligations employees have to employers (and vice versa), and other work-related opinions and values. By satisfying an employee's Parent, a supervisor releases his energy from internal conflict—making it available for productive activity.

Different strokes for different folks

Satisfying a particular employee's Parent requires some preliminary observation. You may notice, for example, that a worker with a very critical Parent makes concessions to it through excessive work—when he doesn't, he loses his peace of mind. Another employee's Critical Parent may demand competitiveness at all times; still another's may dictate that the worker must feel a sense of purpose and satisfaction in working. Thus, Parent tapes may require a wide range of commitment to work as such—from very little to a great deal. The degree of commitment involved will inevitably determine the measures necessary to motivate a subordinate. Some, for example, may never be satisfied in the work they are doing; attempts to enrich their work by making it more challenging, difficult, or responsible merely turn them off. On the whole, though, job enrichment has proved a success—in part, at least, because many people please their Parent by valuing things the Parent values; our society is, after all, still a work- and achievement-oriented one.

Enriching his job usually satisfies a worker's Parent because it allows him to assume more responsibility for his actions, to achieve more, to become more productive—in short, to *make good*. The effect of this is to help reduce interior conflict between Parent and Child. The Parent admonition to the Child—"You should do more with your life"—is answered by the Adult: "My employer recognizes this; I am being given more responsibility and authority." This brings self-approval and relaxes tensions. The desire to do and be more fuels the upward-mobility aspirations of many workers today.

For the Adult, the sense of challenge that comes of being entrusted to do a difficult job is an important motivator. When an employee must stretch to do a little more than he thought possible, he will not only grow with success, but enjoy a sense of renewed confidence in his Adult capability. Additionally, he receives strokes from his supervisor in the form of praise and recognition—very rewarding in themselves. The realization that he can think on his own feet, that he can handle himself well in a demanding situation, makes him feel good. Increased attention to a job's "thinking" requirements, always an important consideration in enriching a job, involves giving a subordinate a variety of stimulating and more difficult tasks. The fact that it calls on him to share in decisions affecting his work exercises his Adult and reassures his Parent.

Taking care of the Child

Since the Child is the primary source of our feelings about ourselves, the work we are given to do must strengthen its sense of OKness. This comes of being able to succeed, not by experiencing repeated failures. A series of failures can result, for example, when a person is developed too rapidly or is underqualified for what he is doing. An employee with Not OK feelings about himself will also be frustrated and held back by a supervisor whose behavior is largely Critical Parent. Of course, this is in general true for everyone. But it is likely to have a sharper, more permanent impact on the development of employees who are least prepared to cope with such an unfortunate experience. The supervisor who tends to "come on" with his Critical Parent may not tolerate mistakes in learning or may expect too much or too little. Unless both supervisor and worker draw upon more Adult behavior, their relationship will remain a one-way situation, leaving the employee a passive recipient, a puppet on a string. The ultimate consequences will be psychological game playing and/or withdrawal. Once an employee withdraws, he moves beyond the reach of job enrichment or any other form of motivation; he stops growing in his job. The opposite occurs when the supervisor has an effective style of leadership. Then the employee moves from withdrawal toward involvement, increasing his sense of OKness.

On any job, the Child is the source of creativity. For its creativity to grow or even remain functional, the Child needs to exercise its abundant curiosity. Many job activities lend themselves to the exercise of creativity. The roots of work simplification, for example, develop in a creative frame of mind that permits fresh viewpoints or novel thinking about traditional methods. Creative thinking facilitates almost any kind of planning and problem solving.

Few people would question the value of being able to produce a lot of ideas or alternatives. Brainstorming groups make exclusive use of each member's Child in order to produce a lot of ideas. This technique absolutely forbids criticism or critical thinking on the part of any member's Parent or Adult while the group is working to generate ideas. Only after a sufficient quantity of new ideas emerges does the group begin to use the collective Adult to evaluate them objectively.

The Child is also the affectionate part of the personality that can make it easier for people to get together and build friendships. When we separate people who are part of a strong informal group—perhaps by erecting cubicles around them—these relationships suffer and morale often drops. People need to socialize and share feelings on a Child-Child friendship basis. Modern motivational programs recognize this by forming work groups based on common tasks or assembly operations and locating people in physical proximity to each other. The need to socialize is quite strong in some people; many consider job friendships to be a primary source of satisfaction in employment. Such people may find it intolerable to work for a supervisor who is unable to express feelings from his Child—who forever comes on all Parent or all Adult. His psychological distance disturbs them.

It's important to remember that people want to be liked as well as accepted and utilized properly. Between any two people, the greater the number of communication paths between their ego states, the longer lived and more satisfactory their relationship is likely to be. That is, when they are both "cooking on all burners," their common interests let them enjoy good rapport. If a breakdown occurs on one level, others are open. In a large hierarchical organization, incidentally, such mutually satisfactory relationships promote efficiency in getting work done despite barriers that the organizational structure may erect. The same, of course, holds true within smaller working groups. In an environment where people have no rapport with each other, one danger is that they will turn their creativity against the organization or against each other in self-defeating conflict.

It's clear, then, that the supervisor who would motivate subordinates must appeal to—must "deal" in—feelings. One way to see clearly how feelings are used and abused is to think of them as trading stamps like the ones you can get when you buy something at certain stores. When you get them, you can either redeem them quickly for a small item that strikes your fancy or you can save them up until you have enough to get something "big."

Stamps of all colors

We use feelings in much the same way. Because we do, TA compares feelings to trading stamps. Muriel James and Dorothy Jongeward have identified blue stamps for depression, brown for feeling inadequate, white for blamelessness, red for anger, gold for good feelings. We all collect feelings in our contacts with others. We collect such stamps at work, at home, everywhere we go. Like trading stamps, they can be cashed on the spot, or we can save them up to fill a few stampbooks. We can choose to express our feelings when they are small, and get them out of our system, or we can let them pile up until we explode at someone. Turning in an accumulation of red stamps can be quite costly—when, for example, we "take it out" on subordinates, pounce on the secretary, give the boss what he has coming, tell personnel what the company can do with the job, etc.

Listening has long been touted as an important social skill for any manager because it allows subordinates to ventilate such feelings (turn in their stamp collection) while the feelings, or collections, are still small. The manager who listens effectively accepts the expression of feelings because he knows that they are not something to be held in contempt or to be ashamed of. In fact, he wants to contend with them early on, because he knows that if he ignores them, he'll only find them expressed in some distorted form later on.

Let them collect gold stamps

Supervisors interested in motivating subordinates through the job or work afford every opportunity for them to collect gold stamps on the job. By doing work that is rewarding for their Parent, Adult, and Child ego states, they collect good feelings. When their supervisor further strokes or rewards them for the good work they do, their self-confidence and sense of OKness increases—more gold stamps—and their proficiency increases apace. Briefly, the two primary sources of gold stamps are satisfaction from doing the job and recognition for doing the job well. The resulting good feelings reinforce the actions that produced them and lead to still higher levels of performance.

Reinforcement: actions and feelings

A supervisor's motivation efforts, then, should center on getting a subordinate started in an upward spiral where feelings and actions reinforce each other. Lacking job satisfaction and recognition, the subordinate's growth stops—he is not able to reach any kind of self-fulfillment through job performance. People who are dissatisfied with their work collect red, blue, and brown stamps—which lead nowhere in terms of employee development. The negative feelings accumulate by the "bookful" and result in serious consequences. Here are a few of the ways in which they find expression:

- Employee game playing and conflicts develop.
- Manhours are wasted.
- Products/services deteriorate.
- Customer relations turn sour.
- The production of constructive ideas withers away.

Put simply, Not OK feelings toward self and others increase, and the work place becomes an exchange center for negative feelings. Have you ever worked with someone who collected blue stamps every day? You probably collected a few just by being near that person. Each of us has a favorite color in our stamp collection. We collect more of some colors than others and, again, the sizes of our collections vary.

When we're under a lot of pressure, we collect and cash in stamps more rapidly as our Adult is "squeezed." Under great pressure—for example, in a tough, short-fused project where error could result in the loss of a job, a promotion, or a customer—we may become so disoriented that we fail. That is, under such pressure, old tapes may take over our thinking. We feel anxious, confused, and angry at ourselves. The Parent steps in with a barrage of such critical remarks as: "You should have been better prepared for this." "If you had trained your people better, you wouldn't be in this mess." "You never were much of a planner." The Child sulks, worries, and feels inadequate: "I know I'm going to fail." "This is too much for me." "It isn't fair." "Maybe I'm in the wrong line of work." "Maybe I ought to quit." Meanwhile, the Adult is hard put even to get a thought in. There is simply no computer time available. It's easy to see the possibilities for stamp collecting here. Under the circumstances, we're ready to accept as valid any negative stroke being dished out.

Feeling rackets

A word of caution for the supervisor who is affecting and being affected by the feelings of other employees: Watch out for racketeers! A racketeer is a person who exploits others in some illegitimate, covert way in order to satisfy his own selfish ends. A feeling racketeer does essentially the same thing. It is one thing to be a feeling, responding person who is subject to real anger, joy, and other legitimate emotions—but it is quite another to seek out bad feelings in order to manipulate people. The term *feeling racket* applies to the way in which a person zaps others or maneuvers them to zap *him* (not necessarily consciously) so that he can manipulate them by playing Persecutor or Victim. Gamesters do this all the time. They take measures to exaggerate "the grief that others cause them" and they look to others for sympathy.

A manager must be able to differentiate between feelings that are appropriate to what has gone on and those that are distorted. He'll have to use his Adult to find out when an employee's collected stamps are real and when they are just figments of the imagination. Many people get into habits of collecting certain feelings, of course, because doing so helps confirm their life positions. Some seem to need to feel guilty, or without fault, or righteous in their "martyrdom." People who get satisfaction from such feelings are said to be in a feeling racket.

Now, you could say that such people are motivated. They certainly are—to achieving ulterior goals! But these goals are not in the best interest of the individual or the organization as a whole. To leave the way clear for productive motivation, we need to learn to make "computer time" for the Adult—i.e., give the Adult a chance to operate. And we need to start exchanging gold stamps. The supervisor who is able to give gold stamps and stimulate others to give and collect them will ultimately be able to build them into a solid currency in his department. By and large, the emphasis will be on good feelings through honest, aboveboard transactions. Only in such an atmosphere can workers feel free to achieve their highest potential.

Counseling

Even under conditions that yield high motivation, however, an occasional worker may for one reason or another have trouble achieving high performance. The trouble may lie in inadequate training, a poor fit between his skills and his job, a seemingly intractable personality conflict, or some other reason. Whatever the reason, you must step in with counseling to alleviate the trouble—and TA techniques can help you do so effectively.

Counseling from the TA viewpoint is a series of transactions designed to improve performance, solve a personal or job-related problem, or develop a path for growth and development. The counseling interview is used to solicit and exchange information, thoughts, and feelings bearing on a problem situation.

TA techniques help broaden our understanding of the important internal events that underlie such encounters. Through transactional analysis, we learn to deal with emotions as well as thoughts—a procedure crucial to successful counseling. During a counseling interview, you have to deal with your own Parent, Adult, and Child as well as those of the employee.

The authority relationship between you and your subordinate poses certain difficulties for some kinds of counseling transactions. There is, for example, the continuing danger that the supervisor's Parent may come on heavy—dominating, intimidating, or patronizing the employee. When this happens, the employee is likely to be frightened or enticed into responding exclusively from his Child—thereby preventing any constructive Adult involvement or commitment. "Whatever you say" replaces "Try to see it from my point of view"—and the interview fails. The supervisor must become aware of his prevailing way of interacting with the employee so that he can take any necessary measures to activate his Adult. On the other hand, he may be *so* Adult-oriented that he seems personally unconcerned and aloof—a position guaranteed to produce a sterile interchange. Let's examine TA's role in the counseling process.

Before the interview

Before a counseling interview, the supervisor will use his time wisely by informing his Adult of necessary facts and considerations. In addition, he may want to examine any Parent or Child programming he has that may make him critical toward the employee or cause him distress in dealing with the employee. By surfacing any anxiety or prejudice involved, he will strengthen his Adult for the task ahead. After this internal review, the Adult can prepare for the interview by examining external files and records that apply.

Knowing the employee's typical response patterns will also help. Consider how you will deal with the employee who has a Not OK view of himself or of you. Be prepared to establish the rapport so necessary in counseling and anticipate ways of getting around any sore points that may interfere with your transactions. Having done these things, you can define your objectives for the counseling interview. If it is intended to change employee behavior, you should have a clear image of how the employee will act after his behavior changes. Define yardsticks for measuring success. Ask yourself, "How will I know when the problem is solved—for him, for me?" "What will things be like at that time?" We often act without an answer to these questions. Trying to answer them will help you spot areas of your ignorance, possible prejudices, wishful thinking, and just plain ill-considered objectives.

If you have a tendency to play Rescuer, ask yourself whether this is truly in the employee's interest. A primary counseling goal is to help the employee stand on his own two feet, to use his Adult successfully. Are you prepared for this to happen? Do you really want this to happen? Check out your "rescuing" motivation. Is it real, or are you doing it merely for personal aggrandizement? One game played by manipulative Rescuers is called "I'm Only Trying to Help You." If you suspect yourself of being this kind of gamester, you might prepare your Child so that it won't be offended when your advice isn't accepted. The best preventive measure, however, is simply to refrain from giving advice. People rarely want or follow outside advice that they haven't internalized to their own satisfaction. What you really want to do is to get the employee to be responsible for his own actions. You are successful when you help him to be his own rescuer. This process is called employee development.

The interview

To put the employee at ease, start by engaging him in a short period of discussion about things that interest him. You can relax his Child by being open and friendly and by announcing the purpose of the interview. Taking an informal tone of voice and posture also helps. Arms folded across chest, hands tinkering with something on the desk, a vacant, disinterested stare, etc., will put him off. Some supervisors establish a better basis for rapport by moving out from behind their desks to align themselves closer with the employee. The following list of do's and don'ts is designed to help you take it from there.

● *Don't try to change his/her personality*. You can't change the content of the employee's ego states. You *can* help him to become aware of their content and elicit his Adult response in mediating his thinking and behavior. Once you do this, you're practically home free.

● *Hold your Parent and Child in check*. Don't fall into a closed Parent-Child transaction in which your Parent tells his Child what to do. Learn to control your Parent and Child while listening. Let him express himself. Don't shoot out loaded questions that corner or trap him. Two games played from the Critical Parent ego state are CORNER, where the employee is trapped no matter what he says, and NIGYSOB. Another game sometimes used in combination with CORNER to trap the employee into a position in which he appears to be at fault is the YES, BUT game. Sometimes the game crops up in performance appraisals, especially when a supervisor's overly critical Parent harbors unrealistic performance expectations. However, the game can easily be played by the person being evaluated, as we shall see later on. In the following example, the boss is calling the shots.

Boss: "On the whole, you've made some progress since the last rating period, but you've certainly got a long way to go."

Employee: "I thought I was doing well. I met all the objectives we set."

Boss: "Yes, but meeting objectives is a minimal achievement. That's expected."

Employee: "Where is it you feel that I've fallen down?"

Boss: "Well, for one thing I don't think you plan your time very well."

Employee: "I never miss a deadline."

Boss: "Yes, but you're missing the point. And here's another thing— you're not very cooperative."

Employee: "I don't understand why you say that. I work well with others."

Boss: "You may be *friendly* with others, but there have been times when you seemed reluctant to accept additional assignments."

Employee: "Well, after all, I *was* busy."
Boss: "Yes, but if you planned your work efficiently, you'd have more time—wouldn't you?"

Here, the employee is cut off from any avenue of retreat. Of course, it's easier to "fix" such a game so he can't win if you have neglected to set performance standards or develop a job description. To avoid playing such a game, learn to disregard Parent messages that may be telling you such things as, "Listen, friend, you shouldn't feel that way" or Child messages that prompt you to say, "If you knew the problems I have, you wouldn't bring me yours." Don't cross-examine or patronize: "Sure you're sore, but look how long it took *me* to make it in this company." This Child reaction is usually followed by a "right hook" from the Parent: "You know, you should be more patient . . . more thankful for the progress you've made here."

• *Avoid admonishing the subordinate.* Admonitions are Parent judgments that take such forms as "You've got the wrong attitude," "You've got to change your ways," "You don't know what's good for you," "If you had taken your education seriously, your career wouldn't be stalled at this point." These have the effect of intimidating the employee's Child and increasing the likelihood of childlike behavior—which may range from pouting to denial and rebellion.

• *Don't discount the employee's feelings and problems.* Instead of helping the employee, remarks like "You don't really have a problem" tend to hook his Child into action with counterremarks or a withdrawal into angry silence. Discounting occurs whenever a person is made to feel that he is being put down, put off, ignored, underrated. The addition of sarcasm makes a particularly biting discount.

• *Don't supply the expected payoff in games.* It takes two or more people to play a game. If you have reason to believe that you are co-starring in some game, you can stop it cold by not offering the expected payoff. In the game of STUPID, for example, the obvious payoff is for you to put the employee down by implying or actually telling him that he's stupid. Simply refuse to do this. If you continue to use your Adult, chances are that the employee will feel incongruous in using his Child and will sooner or later start transacting from his Adult. Realizing that a deep need for recognition underlies much game playing, you can set up conditions in which gold stamps are sought rather than the bad feelings that culminate from game playing. An employee who repeatedly comes to work late or always turns in projects that are too little and too late is angling for a hard putdown in the form of a spoken or written admonition. You know that what he basically wants is recognition, attention. Try to swing him over into a cycle of positive strokes and productive actions. In any event, you should discuss his behavior with him before it reaches the disciplinary level. Remember to use your Adult and call upon his to map out a satisfactory plan for change.

● *Help the employee satisfy his Parent.* This is particularly necessary in order to help some hard-driving self-starters who seem unable to enjoy their successes or take a work break now and then. They find it difficult to relax because their Parent hounds them on to endless activity—even perfection. It may help to establish standards of sufficiency in work performance to keep them from "gilding the lily." Communicating expectations and giving timely recognition for achievement will help in most cases.

● *Give feedback.* From time to time, repeat in your words what the employee says; state the feelings that you think underlie his comments. This shows that you understand his or her feelings and that you consider them to be legitimate and acceptable. Such indications help comfort the employee's Child and activate his Adult. Specific feedback on performance during an appraisal can strengthen the employee's ability to test reality and feel competent in coping with his environment. It helps because it gives him objective measures of his performance against established standards. Generalities don't help an employee grow. What is needed is an action plan for change and development. Simply saying, "You're doing OK in all respects," may even make the employee feel discounted because he feels that you don't care enough to be specific. Honest, specific information on performance can give an employee a sense of increased OKness if it is provided tactfully. Straight, honest evaluations are positive strokes in themselves—because they reflect close attention to the employee's growth.

● *Stroke for being as well as for doing.* Everyone likes to know that he is valued and accepted for himself, not exclusively for what he accomplishes at work. In giving positive strokes for the person, you recognize that there is a great deal more to him than is evident in task-related transactions and activities. The daily rituals of greeting and the pastimes people engage in during informal periods and breaks provide opportunities for this. A sincere expression of interest in how the employee is doing in his schoolwork, family activities, hobbies, or other interests will give strokes that value the person for being a special individual.

• *Keep your transactions straight.* Say what you mean and mean what you say. Avoid innuendo and ulterior transactions. If you say ''That's a promising idea, John'' or ''Your chances of promotion are good'' without meaning it, you are discounting the employee by giving crooked (deceptive) strokes.

• *When reprimanding, separate the person from the act.* When it's necessary to take disciplinary action, address yourself to the behavior involved, not to the personality or presumed attitudes of the employee. Doing this helps you use your Adult to the exclusion of your Parent. In turn, it tends to disarm the employee's Child by making it easier for him to focus on the behavior in question rather than brood on the threat to his self-esteem.

• *Check out the employee's stamp collection.* Is he getting enough gold stamps from his work? From his working relationships? Does he seem to have a favorite color in his stamp collection? How long has he been collecting? Ask yourself what you can do and what he can do to reduce the red and blue stamps and increase the gold.

• *Use your Child in empathizing with him or her.* It is possible to use both your Adult and your Child to convey a sense of understanding an employee's thoughts and feelings from his or her perspective. This is a kind of ''putting yourself in the other person's ego states.'' It doesn't guarantee instant empathy, but it's a better approach to understanding an employee's position than relying on Adult reasoning alone.

• *Enlist his Adult in recognizing his unrealistic wishes and fantasies.* Properly designed questions can help you do this. Sometimes a question can shake a person from lethargy into Adult awareness and commitment. For example, ''What are you doing at this time to further your education so that you can be considered for promotion?'' Too often, people harbor dreams of advancement but fail to act to make those dreams materialize. Some rely heavily on fantasies; like Cinderella, they pass their time waiting for someone or something to rescue them from dead-end jobs, underutilization, and prolonged discontent. Another question that has proved helpful: "What do you think you'll be doing with us three years from now?"

• *Be an active listener.* Being listened to is a highly rewarding experience. In giving our full, undivided attention, we not only provide strokes that encourage the employee to talk more freely and express himself more completely, we also make him feel that he is important, that what happens to him matters. Such listening is an important preliminary to a change in behavior because it allows the employee to ventilate his feelings and put his thoughts together in a more precise and reasonable way. It helps him gain the approval of his Parent ("It was good that you told it like it is") and satisfy his Child ("Gee, he really cares about my feelings").

• *Listen for messages from the employee's Child.* Phrases such as "I can't," "I won't," "I should," "I try, but" signal expressions that probably originate in his Child. They can tell you a great deal about his self-image, his hopes and fears, his doubts and uncertainties. The frequency of such Child expressions signals his degree of difficulty in communicating from his Adult. Consider whether such a difficulty springs from your relationship with him or from the circumstances that led to the interview.

• *Counter the evasive strategy of the employee's manipulative Child.* It may deliberately misinterpret your comments to evade the real issue and get its own way. Where this is a problem, simply have the employee repeat back to you his understanding of what you have said until it's clear that he *does* understand.

• *Don't let periods of silence threaten your Child.* Silence is a device that helps draw the employee out. It also gives you an opportunity to put your thoughts and feelings in order. Some supervisors get distressed when conversation stops. Their Parent may begin to send out such messages as "This shouldn't be happening," "You haven't organized this thing!" "You're putting the poor guy on the spot." These messages may pressure the supervisor to start speaking—but if he does, he's not likely to get to the heart of the employee's feelings and thoughts. He may even maneuver himself into a communication pattern in which the employee simply answers *yes* or *no* to questions without elaborating.

• *Hook the Child's need to be creative.* You might consider assigning him a special report, membership on special task-force committees, or research on new operating procedures; all are capable of allowing him to express his creativity on the job.

• *Maintain your Adult in setting goals even when the opposition is stiff.* The following extract from a counseling interview shows a supervisor making effective use of his Adult in combating the machinations of a subordinate skilled at playing YES, BUT.

Boss: "Sam, I'd like to talk to you about your work. Will you join me in my office?"

Sam: "Oh, okay, I'll be right with you."

Boss: "I'll come right to the point. Your work has been deteriorating recently. Your productivity has fallen off and you've failed to meet three deadlines."

Sam: "My work is as good as ever."

Boss: "I'm not talking about how well you do things. I'm referring to how *much* you do and how *quickly* you do them."

Sam: "Well, ever since we had to start using the new set-up procedure, nobody has been doing as much as before."

Boss: "Sam, everyone in the section was consulted for their opinions before we installed it—including you. Nobody expressed any objections. It you want to talk about the production of the others, take a look at this production chart first."

Sam: "Well, okay—so *they're* doing fine, but this new set-up throws *me* off."

Boss: "Sam, your production started dropping before we began the new procedure."

Sam: "Well, believe me, the new set-up procedure didn't help. Anyway, as they say, you can't teach an old dog new tricks."

Boss: "Didn't your team leader explain it all to you?"

Sam: "Yes, he did—but I guess I just didn't get it."

Boss: "He told me he spent several hours with you."

Sam: "I suppose he did—maybe I'm just thick."

Boss: "We'll give you whatever assistance you need to understand it. If necessary, I'll arrange to streamline the production procedure on your line. Now, what about the deadlines, Sam—that's another matter."

Sam: "Yes, but I can't possibly meet them with all these changes taking place."

Boss: "Sam, you can take measures to make yourself more effective. I will do what I can to remove barriers to your performance. I'm setting up another meeting with you to go over positive measures that you can take to meet production standards. I expect you to. . . ."

The boss's closing remarks show that he is making effective use of his Adult. He has not been taken in or confused by Sam's excuses. He has promised to remove possible barriers to performance and he is making it clear that he means business. Throughout all this he has "kept his cool" (remained in his Adult). He has refrained from discounting Sam. To give Sam a chance to start responding from *his* Adult, he is setting up a meeting to examine the measures he expects Sam to design and Sam to execute.

Successful counseling interviews occur when both supervisor and subordinate leave with a common understanding of their responsibilities and a genuine commitment to follow through. To assure this, the wise supervisor conducts follow-up evaluations as a control measure to determine whether the goals were practical and to see whether the action being taken will assure their attainment.

References and Recommended Reading on Transactional Analysis

ERIC BERNE:
Transactional Analysis in Psychotherapy, Grove Press, N.Y., 1961.
Games People Play, Grove Press, N.Y., 1964.
What Do You Say After You Say Hello? Grove Press, N.Y., 1972.

THOMAS HARRIS:
I'm OK—You're OK, Harper, N.Y., 1969.

MURIEL JAMES AND DOROTHY JONGEWARD:
Born to Win: TA with Gestalt Experiments, Addison-Wesley, Mass., 1971.

Communicating with Subordinates

Revised Edition / Edited by Thomasine Rendero

James M. Lahiff

Clear Up Communication Static

ACCORDING TO the United States Treasury Department, there are three types of workers: the ones who make things happen, the ones who watch things happen, and the ones who don't know what happened.

The supervisor who "makes things happen" realizes that communication is at the core of most supervisory problems and works to facilitate the communication process every day. He is conscious of the many variables that influence the people around him and takes all these variables into account whenever he interacts with his subordinates. He knows that communication is a human transaction subject to the usual human frailties and that human obstacles confront all people who want to communicate with one another.

If you are a supervisor who wants to achieve total communication, you should consider the total environment in which your subordinates operate. You should try to become sensitive to their feelings, social needs, and the physical and psychological field in which they work. If you master both roles in an information exchange, you can become a clear transmitter and an understanding listener.

Here is an analysis of the many factors that influence com-

Assistant Professor, Department of Management, The University of Georgia

munication. Consider these elements the next time you want to "make things happen."

Communication breakdowns

Traditionally, most breakdowns in communication have been attributed to one of three causes:

1. *The deficiencies of the sender.* Because the sender is the most visible agent, he is usually blamed for a breakdown in communication. When there is evidence of ineffective oral communication, the sender may be charged with such transgressions as lack of clarity or not enough volume. Such comments as, "He's so vague," or "She's so disorganized," are familiar criticisms leveled at senders.

2. *The listener's lack of responsibility.* Frequently, the listener is accused of not having done his part. Conflicting demands on a supervisor's time and attention are commonly cited as reasons for faulty listening. The fact that few supervisors ever receive any training in listening makes most of them fair game for such a charge. As long as listening continues to be regarded as a passive, naturally acquired skill, poor listening will continue to be widespread.

3. *Inappropriate means of communication.* You may send a memo, for example, when the message could have been transmitted more clearly by telephone or face-to-face. In some organizations, the communication channels are so overloaded with memos that in order to get someone to notice a memo, the sender may have to employ other means—and the other means may not necessarily be suited to the particular message.

Since people have a tendency to pattern their behavior after others, most members of an organization will eventually mirror one another in communication practices. There is much to be said in favor of a unique approach. Unfortunately, this quality is not nurtured in the average organizational environment.

Be a better listener

Selecting an appropriate means of communicating and making sure that the communication—whether it is oral or written—has been clearly stated are relatively difficult tasks compared with becoming an able listener. Research has shown that our hearing ability is more highly developed than is our speaking ability. We are physically able to comprehend four or five times as many words per minute as we are able to speak.

It would seem that the listener has a natural advantage over the speaker. Human nature being what it is, however, this apparent advantage has become a handicap, because most of us actually use this advantage for nonproductive purposes. Think for a minute how you use "spare time" when you are listening. Most people either daydream or think of what the speaker is going to say next. When two such non-communicators interact, what ensues is a "duolog." A "duolog," according to Richard M. Greene, Jr., author of *The Management Game,* is "when two people take turns not talking to each other." Since each concentrates on only his own thoughts, there is little likelihood of achieving mutual understanding.

Carl Rogers, the renowned authority on counseling, feels that too many of us use this "spare time" to evaluate what is being said. He considers this evaluation to be the main barrier to communication—because when we evaluate, we are concentrating on our own feelings toward the speaker. Instead, our attention should be focused on the sender and the meaning of his message. When we evaluate a message while it is still being sent, we are acting without sufficient evidence. And we'll never get sufficient evidence, because we are not listening.

Become an analyst

The introduction of the instant replay to televised football games has resulted in the transformation of millions of spectators to the elevated rank of analysts. Prior to the advent of the instant replay, most sports fans were quite unsophisticated. Individual plays progressed at a rapid pace, and the viewer was forced to concentrate on the ball carrier's progress or lack of progress. With the instant replay, the viewer can scrutinize each play's development, become aware of the individual assignments that are being carried out and, over the course of several series of plays, become able to recognize the opposing quarterback's strategies.

An effective listener has the same sort of capability. Within each of us is an instant replay mechanism—and it is the ability to use this that separates the listeners from the hearers. A listener uses "spare time'' to reorganize the speaker's message—while the person is speaking. In this restructuring process, he constructs a mental outline of the message that he replays in his mind. He searches for the speaker's main idea, then looks for the ways in which the speaker supports the main idea.

The unwillingness to listen

Inability to listen is easier to cure than unwillingness to listen. Often the unwillingness to listen is grounded in obstinacy rather than ignorance. When, for example, the unwilling listener is the communicator's superior, he may erect his status as a barrier to communication.

WHY THEY TUNE YOU OUT *By Roger D'Aprix*

DO YOU EVER get the feeling that your subordinates can't understand plain English? Maybe they subconsciously tune you out because you rub them the wrong way.

Mark Brodstreet, for example, is a manager of technical budgets and expenses for LaFayette Aerodynamics. Technical cost analyst Leonardo Schultz reports to him. Communication between these two people is deplorable.

Part of the problem is that Leonardo was originally trained as an engineer and learned his cost accounting in night school. Brodstreet is a CPA with no technical training. He is forever holding forth in Leonardo's presence that engineers are an inferior breed with no conception of cost or profit.

For his part, Leonardo believes in the notion of ''the whole man,'' and he feels that anyone who is monitoring costs should have a basic understanding of design and of the impact of cost cuts on the final product.

Recently, Leonardo supported a group of design engineers who protested Brodstreet's edict that 20 percent of the material cost had to be pruned from a new braking system for jet aircraft. In the middle of a group discussion, Brodstreet lost his temper, abruptly ended the meeting, and stated that he was going to carry the whole matter to the vice-president of engineering.

Privately, he read the riot act to Leonardo and accused him of being

Sometimes, unwillingness to listen could have been prevented if the communicator had done some advance planning. For instance, Lloyd Duncan wanted to talk to his supervisor, Mo Murphy, about the increase in unredeemable scrap materials. Mo made an appointment with Lloyd for 9:30, but he rushed impatiently through the meeting because he had made another appointment with his own supervisor for 9:45. If Mo had exercised more care in scheduling the meetings, Lloyd wouldn't have gotten the impression that Mo couldn't have cared less.

If a person feels that a topic threatens his ego, he may also be unwilling to listen. When Jack Price, supervisor in the shipping department, tried to discuss Bob Sack's substandard job performance, he met with understandable resistance. But when Jack approached Bob's

---

"a frustrated engineer who couldn't make a living at it." He finished the confrontation by questioning Leonardo's "two-bit night-school accounting degree" and reminding him that his first loyalty was to Brodstreet and not to a bunch of spendthrift engineers. They haven't spoken to each other for two weeks now, except to carry on the most essential and rudimentary communication.

Where did the relationship go awry? Brodstreet trampled on one of the basic principles of good human relations. Simply stated: Communication is difficult between two people who do not like or respect one another.

This is not to say that if you are going to communicate successfully, you must be liked at all costs. But successful communication does require concentration and a minimum of distraction. If somebody doesn't like you or doesn't trust or respect you or your judgment, it's easy for him to be distracted by his dislike or distrust. Thus, he tends not to hear (or believe) anything you tell him.

Brodstreet attacked Leonardo as a professional and as a person, and the recollection of that attack is practically the only thing that Leonardo will "hear" whenever Brodstreet talks to him.

The lesson is clear: If you want to communicate, you must win and hold the other person's goodwill and respect. This means that you can criticize his actions or his ideas, but you should never attack his self-esteem or his ego.

—*Reprinted from Machine Design, December 28, 1972. Copyright 1972 by The Penton Publishing Company, Cleveland, Ohio.*

performance as only one of several causes of low departmental output, Bob was much more willing to listen.

Watch the field

While the sender, receiver, and means of communication are the elements most often blamed for communication failures, there are other possibilities. Among these other variables, "the field" is most often overlooked. The field is the environment in which the communication attempt is made. Two different types of fields can be distinguished: the physical and the psychological. The physical field is easily visible to participants. Such features as the size of the room, illumination, and furnishings are part of this field.

Lack of awareness of the physical field can sometimes lead to embarrassment or worse. If Charlie Johnson had known that Mark Bloom, County Chairman of the Democratic Party, was on the other side of the file cabinet, he undoubtedly would have swallowed his denunciation of the Democratic platform. Unfortunately, he didn't have the complete picture of the physical field in which he was communicating.

Here is an example of a supervisor who wasn't perceptive about the physical field:

Nancy Thornton, supervisor in word processing, approached two of her subordinates while they were taking their coffee break in the lounge. She asked them about the progress of a work order that personnel had sent down that day and asked them to get it out as soon as possible. The next day, when the order still wasn't out, she reprimanded them for having failed to get it out right away.

In this incident, the supervisor didn't perceive the physical field in the same way the workers did. Since the workers were seated in comfortable, relatively quiet surroundings, the supervisor considered it an ideal opportunity to pass on some orders to them.

But *they* perceived it quite differently. They felt that the purpose of the lounge was to give them a place in which they could relax and "get away from it all" for a short time, and they resented Nancy's intrusion. Nancy failed to consider the setting from the point of view of her subordinates.

This is a common mistake. The supervisor who tries to give orders to a subordinate while that subordinate is operating a machine is not only misperceiving the field, but—most likely—violating safety regulations. The door-to-door salesman who calls during the dinner hour and the office manager who reprimands a subordinate within earshot of co-workers are also misperceiving the field. Even worse is the foreman who tries to explain a new company policy to a worker waiting to punch out at the time clock.

The psychological field

The psychological field is a composite of such unseen influences as the attitudes of the participants and the amount of tension in a particular situation. This field, of course, is less readily apparent than the physical field.

In the "coffee caper," the attitudes of the workers toward Nancy would determine their readiness to accept orders during their coffee break. If she were well liked by her staff, she would be more likely to have her orders accepted than if she were detested. If such an intrusion were unusual for her, it would suggest urgency and thus motivate the workers to cooperate with her.

Each supervisor determines to a great extent his subordinates' psychological field. If his staff feels that he is fair, they will tolerate a greater invasion of their psychological field than if they feel that he is capricious, deliberately unfair, or cruel. While it isn't possible to become completely aware of all the influences affecting subordinates, a perceptive supervisor can learn to identify and cope with many of them.

Feedback

Feedback is essential in any communication process. An effective communicator effectively uses all available feedback. He observes incoming feedback and tries to adapt his response to its message. For example, a public speaker who notices all his listeners leaning forward during his speech will adapt to that message by speaking louder.

Too often, supervisors become oblivious to feedback. Those who have become rooted in a position will grow increasingly inflexible toward and unconcerned about those around them. Such rigidity often results in authoritarian behavior and a philosophy that "my way is the right way, because that's the way I've always done it."

Here is another example of a communication breakdown caused by management's inability to heed feedback: Several years ago, a survey was conducted to determine factors most important to workers' morale. Both supervisors and subordinates were asked to rank ten distinct factors that influenced workers in order of importance. Management ranked the following factors in the bottom three places on their list: full appreciation for work done, feeling "in on things," and sympathetic help on personal problems. In ranking the same ten factors, workers ranked these three factors first, second, and third. Management had been "dead wrong."

This illustrates what can happen when management fails to pay attention to feedback from employees until it is too late. Management often doesn't make provisions for feedback—and even when provision is made, the feedback is frequently ignored.

The amount of feedback that takes place in an organization often determines its "climate." The climate can be described in terms of the company's communication policies—both formal and informal. Use of the term "climate" may suggest that, like the weather, it is beyond human control. But such a connotation is unfortunate, since climate control has long been possible. All the members of an organization—particularly those in positions of leadership—influence its climate.

The meaning is the message

In order to thoroughly analyze the communication process, we must also consider the message. While it is impossible to ever completely disassociate the message from its source, the two *are* separate entities. The fact that a sender is articulate and forthright does not ensure that the message will be comprehensible to the receiver. Only a message that is organized logically and geared to the receiver's level of knowledge will make sense to the receiver. Even knowledge of the sender's high status, which accompanies his written message on its rounds, will not ensure its acceptance.

As you prepare your messages, keep in mind the response you want and the person you want it from. Make sure that the message will be interpreted as you had intended. Most people have, at one time or another, endured an interview whose purpose never emerged. Very often, this is the interviewer's fault because he started transmitting his information before explaining his purpose. The person who does this regularly will acquire a reputation for "going off half-cocked."

Nonverbal communication

In this analysis of communication, written and oral messages have been stressed. But there is another kind of message that supervisors transmit daily. Julius Fast made the public aware of it in his book *Body Language*. Since research findings indicate that no more than 35 percent of our meaning is carried in verbal messages, the important role that nonverbal communication plays cannot be overlooked.

One obvious way in which we communicate nonverbally is through the way we dress. Now that business organizations have liberalized dress standards somewhat, people have greater opportunity for self-expression through dress. While your worth as an employee is not measured by your particular clothing style, you should be aware of the way in which co-workers respond to your clothing. There is no right and wrong way to dress, but there is an image of yourself that you will project through the way you dress. In addition to dress, of course, there are many other avenues of nonverbal communication—ranging from facial expression and personal mannerisms to the kind of car you drive.

The successful salesman, for example, who makes a higher salary and occupies a higher position than those of his customers, may not always flaunt his success. He may—if he is sensitive to the nonverbal message he transmits—choose to drive a moderately priced car and wear simple clothes. Why? To do otherwise may tell his customers, "I'm more successful than you are. I don't need your help anymore." Many once-successful firms have gone downhill because of "executive conceit."

While the salesman may be aware of what he is doing, supervisors too often have little control over their nonverbal expressions. This lack of control often puts them in a self-incriminating position: They are caught in the act of being themselves. Unlike verbal communication in which they can "weigh their words" before speaking or writing, there is no safeguard in nonverbal communication. For that reason, when there is a discrepancy between two messages that you have transmitted—one verbal and one nonverbal—listeners are more likely to accept your nonverbal message. The only way to guard against being caught with "your meaning down" is to become a better listener and pay close attention to feedback.

Don't project

The psychological mechanism called projection, which can play havoc with communication, is shown in the morale survey in which management was guilty of projecting its own feelings onto the workforce. Projection also operates in the area of interviewing and hiring minority group members who may hold values and aspirations different from those of the majority of the workforce.

Empathy, the opposite of projection, facilitates communication. When a supervisor empathizes with a subordinate, he identifies with the subordinate in order to increase his understanding of the subordinate's thoughts and feelings. If the group of managers who participated in the morale study had empathized more with the workers, their recognition of the workers' morale problems would have more closely resembled the workers' own perceptions.

(Reprinted from SUPERVISORY MANAGEMENT, March 1973)

Harold K. Mintz

Memos That Get Things Moving

WHEN YOU SEND a memo, you want to inform recipients, to change their attitude, to get them to take action—in short, to get things moving. The key to writing effective memos is organization, provided that your information is accurate and relevant and your style designed for maximum impact.

Memo organization is not a static, repetitive chore; it changes with the subject and with each group of readers. With one subject, the chronological approach may be most suitable; with another, the question-and-answer approach may be best. One group of readers may prefer the general-to-specific organization; another group may lean toward a cause-and-effect organization.

Whatever kind of organization you choose (based on an assessment of the readers' needs), you should:

- Tell the readers only what they need to know.
- Tell them what it means.
- Tell them what action, if any, to take—and when to take it.

Later on, we will discuss ways of organizing a memo to achieve these objectives.

Communications Specialist, Honeywell Information Systems, Inc.

Memos can move up and down at all levels or sideways across departmental and divisional lines. They can go to one person or hundreds—to superiors, to peers, to subordinates. Occasionally, they may even go to customers, suppliers, and other interested outsiders.

Although memos can run to ten pages or more, short memos—one or two pages—are preferable. In this era of documentation overkill, there is a persuasive argument for brevity. Have your memo typed single-spaced, with double spaces between paragraphs.

The importance of organization

The overall organization of a memo should ensure that it answers basic, relevant questions concerning its subject: What are the facts? What do they mean? What do we do now?

To supply the answers, a memo needs at least some of the following elements: summary, conclusions and recommendations, introduction, main discussion, and closing. Incidentally, these elements make excellent headings to break up the text and alert readers to upcoming topics.

A memo may be well worded and contain all the needed information, but still fail in its objective. Why? Usually the reason is illogical thinking, which results in poor organization characterized by digressions, irrelevancies, and illogical or ineffective sequence of information.

The writer of a good memo keeps his purpose and the reader's needs uppermost in mind; he includes all material bearing upon that purpose and those needs. In addition, he arranges the material in a logical sequence. To meet these requirements, always outline your material before you start writing.

Exhibit 1 shows a poorly organized memo (with real names and dates changed) that was distributed in a "sick" division of a national corporation. At the time, rumors were ricocheting wildly that the division was up for sale; top management was saying nothing. Understandably, morale plummeted. Employees concerned about their jobs were doing little work aside from updating their résumés. This situation was allowed to fester for days before the memo was issued.

Note that the key facts are buried in the fifth paragraph. They should have been headlined and highlighted, as in the reorganized memo (Exhibit 2).

Principles of organization

Logical organization of a memo will help your readers understand the message. To achieve such organization, you must first know the underlying objective of your memo. Then you can proceed to the first two steps: Select all the information relevant to the objective and orga-

---

EXHIBIT 1. ORIGINAL MEMO, WITH NAMES AND DATES CHANGED.

To:	All Managers	**Date**	6–18–72
From:	J. L. Dunphy		
	Medical Instruments	**Telephone**	4321
	Division (MID)		
Subject:	PUBLISHED STATEMENTS CONCERNING POSSIBLE		
	ACQUISITION OF MID BY ZILLION CORPORATION		

On Thursday, June 12, the *Wall Street Financial News Wire* carried the following news item:

"Zillion Corporation said there is absolutely nothing to rumors that it is negotiating to buy ACE's Medical Instruments Division."

In response to inquiries generated by this news item, ACE Corporation has also stated that this rumor has no basis in fact.

Although both Zillion and ACE have stated that there is no substance to this rumor, a number of newspapers, including the *New York Sentinel,* carried the Wall Street news item with the result that many of our employees, customers, suppliers, and others with whom we do business will be exposed to this rumor—either in the form of a denial, as published, or in a distorted form that omits the denial.

In order to preclude further speculation on this subject, I would like to make it clear to you that the management of ACE is definitely not conducting discussions with Zillion and has absolutely no intention of selling its Medical Instruments Division to anyone.

It is important that you convey this fact to the members of your organization, and anyone else you come in contact with, should you be questioned with regard to this rumor.

> J. L. DUNPHY
> *Vice President and General Manager*
> *ACE Medical Instruments Division*

EXHIBIT 2. SAME MEMO REORGANIZED TO HIGHLIGHT THE TWO
KEY FACTS. MEMO IS ALSO "DE-FATTED."

Subject: Facts regarding Rumor of MID Acquisition by Zillion.

Fact 1.   ACE HAS NO INTENTION OF SELLING ITS
MID TO ZILLION CORPORATION OR
ANYONE ELSE.

Fact 2.   ACE is not conducting discussions with Zillion or
anyone else.

I urge you to convey these crucial facts to members of your departments and to anybody who asks about the rumor.

This rumor has appeared in many newspapers. For example, on June 12 the *Wall Street Financial News Wire* carried the following news item: "Zillion Corporation said there is absolutely nothing to the rumor that it is negotiating to buy ACE's Medical Instruments Division." A few days later the *N.Y. Sentinel* published the same item.

As a result of all the publicity, many of our employees, customers, suppliers, and other business associates have been exposed to this damaging rumor.

I consider it the highest priority that you clarify Facts 1 and 2 to everybody concerned.

---

nize the information under major headings arranged in logical sequence.

Here are some approaches to organizing information:

Chronological. A historical account of a project may start at the very beginning, or may start with current happenings and "flash back" to earlier periods.

Geographical. A monthly memo reporting national sales figures may be broken down by regions and states. Other approaches may include: top to bottom, east to west, inside to outside, etc.

Known to unknown or simple to complex. Since you know more about the subject of your memo than your reader does, remember that what is simple to you may be complex to him.

General to specific. Here, you lead off with a general, comprehensive statement and then support it with specific examples. You may also reverse this, going from the specific to the general.

Cause and effect. In this arrangement, you discuss the causes of an event or situation and its effects. If the effects are more dramatic or startling, you may first discuss them and then the causes.

Question and answer. Here, you answer questions to arrive at a desired goal: informing readers, winning their goodwill, or convincing them to do what you want.

The problem, the analysis, the solution. State the problem, analyze it, and give its solution.

Functional. Mechanical or electrical products, for example, may be discussed according to their functions. This principle also applies to the functions of specialists (in marketing, research, product development, etc.).

Most important to least important. Recipients of your memo want to know quickly what is important, why, and what to do about it. That explains why conclusions and recommendations should often be placed at the beginning.

Front matter—essential headings

Every memo contains five essential headings at the top: (1) the name of the firm or company, (2) *To,* (3) *From,* (4) *Subject,* and (5) *Date.* These headings may appear in various sequences and positions.

Name of firm: This should be on all business stationery.

To: Use the recipients' first and last names without *Mr., Mrs.,* or *Ms.,* but with a professional title such as *Dr.* or *Colonel.* If the memo is slated for several people, put their names after the *To* and before the *From.* But if the list is long, put only the primary recipient's name after *To.* The other names can go into a distribution list at the end of the memo.

From: Your name and title go here. In an informal memo, you may omit your title.

Subject. State the subject specifically in a dozen words or fewer, if at all possible. Note that the subject line in Exhibit 1 does not even come close to the employees' basic question: What about us?

Date: All memos require dates.

Front matter—optional headings

The front matter may also contain optional headings: references, memo number, attachments, addresses, and your telephone number.

References. References may be letters, memos, reports, or any other documents that pertain to the subject. If references are needed, number or letter them and give all the information necessary to retrieve them: titles, names of issuing organization and author, publication date, etc. In the memo text, refer to these documents by their assigned numbers or letters.

Attachments (or enclosures). Occasionally, a memo requires such attachments as photographs, tables, calculations, charts, copies of correspondence or contracts, etc. Handle attachments as you do references; see above. (Attachments are also discussed later on under back matter.)

Addresses of writer and readers. In large organizations (say, over 500 employees), spell out departmental and divisional names when departments and divisions are located in different geographical areas. Sometimes departments are assigned mail stop numbers to help expedite mail delivery. These names and numbers will ensure prompt delivery of your memos.

Writer's telephone number. It pays to include your phone number because telephone contact is a quick way to answer questions about your memos. Add your area code whenever necessary.

Elements of memo text

Some of the following elements of memo text are optional.

Summary. Every memo longer than two typed pages should open with a summary, preferably in five to ten lines. The summary should be written after the memo is written, in nontechnical, jargon-free language so that recipients at all levels can understand it. This will help them to decide in seconds whether they want to read the entire memo, a part of it, or just the summary.

Although a summary cannot supply all the facts, it gives their overall meaning and highlights the central idea. Items that belong in a summary include the following, if they are applicable: findings, conclusions, and recommendations. If space allows, procedures and any unusual circumstances may be mentioned.

If you anticipate favorable—or, at best, neutral—reactions to the memo, it's best to place the summary at the very beginning. In that prime position, it will get readers' undivided attention and let them know, quickly, the significance of the memo.

But if you expect a hostile reaction, a summary (especially one that states conclusions and recommendations) at the beginning might turn off many people. Instead, lead off with a statement of the problem or situation, then discuss it objectively (but stressing advantages of your side), and close with conclusions and recommendations. With this approach, you may swing key readers around to your banner by the time they digest your analysis.

Introduction. The primary objective of an introduction is to get the reader ''on board'' so that he can understand the rest of the memo. You can orient him by stating in the first paragraph the purpose of the memo and the importance and scope of its subject. If you think the reader needs more background or a definition of terms, you can add another paragraph (or more) to the introduction.

This approach applies both to one-shot memos and to those that introduce a series of memos. Of course, if a memo is one of a series that has already started, the first sentence should plunge into the ongoing subject.

Many one-shot memos require no introduction at all. Memos announcing meetings, new lunch periods, promotions, vacation policies, transmittal of a document, etc., should state the necessary facts and stop. One paragraph may wrap it up.

Where both a summary and an introduction are appropriate, an alternate arrangement is to lead off with an ''on-board'' type of introduction and then move into a summary. You can, of course, omit from the summary any items covered in the introduction.

Other possible items for an introduction are:

- A question or an answer to a question.
- A thank-you statement.
- A statement of good news or the approval of a proposal.

If the recipient's goodwill is important to you, there are two things to avoid in the first paragraph. Don't say *no;* instead, give him valid reasons for the turndown and, if possible, an alternative course of action. Then the *no* may not sting as much. Also avoid saying that he made a mistake. If you can, first give him a deserved compliment. If that is not possible, you may use the passive voice to salve the recipient's ego: ''The wrong paint was ordered'' rather than ''You ordered the wrong paint.''

Main discussion. The heart of a memo, its main discussion, may range from a few analytical paragraphs to pages of analysis. Although a memo must stick to one subject, the spectrum of subjects is almost unlimited. Here are a few: a new decision; a policy change; a request for information; a complaint or an answer to a complaint; minutes of a meeting; report of a trip.

Facts and figures characterize a main discussion that serves the readers. Information is what they need in order to make a decision or to successfully fulfill any other responsibility.

Here is where organizing skill enables you to marshal the information under various headings: statement of purpose, approach to the problem, account of work done, theory, equipment, methods, results and their analysis (including negative results), conclusions, recommendations, and plans for future work.

Conclusion (*closing*). As used here, the word "conclusion" means the end of a memo, not a decision reached on the basis of findings or results.

If your memo warrants a conclusion—and many do not—the conclusion should be brief and should include no new information or opinion. Since it comes last, it will probably fix the reader's impression of the whole memo. Above all, the conclusion should stress, in new wording, the key idea and perhaps even the attitude that you want the reader to carry away.

Other possible items for a conclusion are a summary of major points, acknowledgment of assistance given, a look-ahead at work to be done, a critical question directed at the reader, a demand or request for action by the reader, or a request for an answer by a certain date.

Back matter—optional elements

The complimentary closes and signatures used in letters are omitted from memos. You may or may not, however, sign your memo.

Distribution list. Memos are extremely flexible in distribution; they may go to one person or 1,000. Most memos, however, are aimed at fewer than a dozen people. In selecting recipients of memos on a long-term project, ask yourself two questions: Are these people involved with the project and, if they are not, should they be kept informed? If either answer is *yes,* add their names to the list. If your answer is not clear-cut, and if you're concerned with only a handful of people, ask them if they want the memos. Remember: You may waste time for your boss if you send him copies of all your memos.

Any memo dealing with a sensitive, controversial, or vitally important topic should, for self-protection, be sent to two or more people. Long after a weighty memo has been distributed, an only recipient who originally favored your position may later oppose you for personal or political reasons and may even claim that he didn't receive your memo. Sending it to others will at least partially disarm the opposition.

The principle of having back-up recipients also applies to any idea that you want to protect as your own. If you devise a new process, product, or marketing strategy, announce it in a memo—with one copy to your boss and copies to others concerned.

Arrangement of list. Names on a distribution list usually appear in alphabetical order, since most people readily accept that order. But if you know the recipients' ranks, you may list them by rank where this seems appropriate.

Placement of distribution list. If the list contains a dozen or fewer names, the logical place for it is after the *To,* provided there is enough room. A dozen names should fit on two lines. If the list is longer than two lines, place it at the end of the memo—but don't forget to reference it after the *To* (for example, *distribution list on page 3*).

Attachments. Attachments should provide evidence that supports and clarifies the subject of the memo. How much of the attachments should be included in the memo proper? Brief quotations or key points, or merely summaries of the attachments? Clear-cut answers depend on the circumstances surrounding the memo and on the readers' needs. Often it is impractical to include a multipage attachment. But including a quotation or photograph or table from an attachment may well multiply the memo's effectiveness.

(Reprinted from SUPERVISORY MANAGEMENT, August 1973)

James Owens

Is Your Communication Lost in Translation?

A GOOD COMMUNICATOR is like a good chess player: He is able to anticipate and identify potential problems before he makes a move. Because of this, he is often able to prevent a communication breakdown. And if something unforeseen should cause a breakdown, he is ready to handle it.

Every supervisor should be a communication expert because he spends 70 percent of his time on the job communicating or trying to communicate through writing, talking, reading, or listening. In order to be 100 percent successful, the supervisor should be able to pinpoint the causes of communication breakdowns. When he can't, these are the kinds of dilemmas that can result:

Harry Morgan complimented his assistant June Schaeffer: "You did this job beautifully, June." To him, his words meant that he appreciated the work and effort she had put into the job. To her, they meant, "You usually do things wrong. This is an improvement." She spent the rest of the day sulking. Could Harry have prevented this misunderstanding? Could he have known how June would react?

It took production supervisor Jacky Horton three days to get a truckload of urgently needed boxes to the right floor of the right build-

Acting Dean, School of Business Administration, The American University

ing at Piermont Chemicals. Why? Because the boxes kept showing up in the wrong place. Imagine the waste and costs that resulted from this bottleneck—the result of a communication breakdown in directions and orders.

Do you know what your biggest communication problems are? Several thousand managers were interviewed over a period of five years to find out what they considered to be the most common—and critical—causes of communication breakdowns. Nine specific communication barriers emerged from the survey. They were:

1. *The difference between communicators in background, experience, or attitudes.* This deeply based barrier between people is a gap that separates one human being and his *meanings* from another because of differences in personality: specifically, differences in background, attitudes, prejudices, beliefs, emotions, opinions, education, experiences, viewpoints, objectives, loves, hates, fears, anxieties, religions, and anything else that constitutes a person's total "life-style."

This gap is the reason that many parents can't communicate well with their children; or whites with blacks; or line people with staff people; or marketing people with production people; or supervisors with subordinates.

For example, Shana Abels, office manager at an insurance company, telephoned Robin Spitz in personnel. "I'd like some information about sick days, please. One of my subordinates asked me about the policy today, and I'm sorry to say that I'm pitifully uninformed. In fact, I couldn't even find it in the company manual."

"Well, I'm sorry, but we just can't give that information out," said Robin.

"Isn't there anything you can tell me?" asked Shana.

"No, you'll just have to look it up in the manual," Robin sighed, making her irritation audible.

Shana was angry and upset. Even worse, she felt frustrated. Why couldn't she get a straight answer? "Those personnel people really think they're important," she thought.

The cause of this communication muddle was that Robin neglected to explain why she couldn't give the information out: If employees knew how many "free" sick days they were allowed, they might take advantage. Shana didn't put herself in Robin's position and was content to blame it on the fact that Robin was one of those "personnel people." Both of them failed to communicate effectively.

Most people who deal with people whom they perceive to be "different" fail to communicate. Why? Because they are so imprisoned in their own viewpoint that they are usually unaware of what the other person is feeling.

• *Remedy: Use empathy.* Empathy means putting yourself in the other person's shoes and trying to see and experience a situation from his or her point of view instead of your own. According to *Webster's,* it is the "projection of yourself into the personality of another in order to understand him better." It is part of the magic that makes human relations work.

The supervisor who forces himself to see the other person's viewpoint will suddenly understand what the other person's reasons are for feeling the way he does. In Shana's and Robin's case, for example, they did not try to understand each other's viewpoint. Robin could have explained her reasons more fully if she had realized that Shana might not be aware of the reasons for her secrecy; Shana could have tried to see the situation from Robin's viewpoint.

2. *People stereotypes.* When you believe that all the members of a group are the same, you are stereotyping them. People usually have built-in positive or negative attitudes that they associate with a stereotyped group, and these attitudes start operating the moment that they come in contact with a member of that group. Sometimes, merely the word *salesman, auditor, New Yorker,* or *organizer* instantly activates mental blocks and defensive thinking to make genuine communication impossible.

• *Remedy: Treat each person as an individual.* Make a conscious effort to ignore stereotyped images. By ignoring programmed prejudgments, you will keep your communication channels open and be able to listen and understand meanings.

3. *Symbols that have different meanings for different people.* Communication is the transfer of meanings between the sender and the receiver. Symbols are only a means to this end. When the sender decides on his meaning, he sends out symbols to the receiver that clearly match the meaning in the sender's mind. But although the sender already knows what his meaning is, the receiver doesn't. Therefore, the receiver is totally dependent on symbols to gain an understanding of the sender's meaning. Unfortunately, symbols often convey meanings that are quite different from what the sender intended.

For example, suppose a salesman tells a potential customer that a refrigerator is "guaranteed." The salesman knows exactly what he means by "guaranteed" because he has years of experience with the detailed mechanics and standard limitations of a guarantee. The customer, on the other hand, only hears the word *guarantee*. Having no knowledge of the real meaning as perceived by the salesman and others who are familiar with the refrigeration industry, the poor customer thinks that if he buys the product, he will be able to get future repairs indefinitely. He buys the refrigerator. The result: Later, when the customer needs repairs, he finds out that they are not covered by the guarantee. The customer probably won't buy from that company again.

The basis for a misunderstanding of symbols is inherent in the communication process because there is a fundamental gap between meanings and symbols. The *Oxford English Dictionary* lists 14,070 different meanings for the 500 most common English words—a ratio of 28 to 1. On the average, any one of these 500 words may have 28 different meanings, depending on the background of the receiver and the context of the situation. The word *round,* for example, has 73 different meanings.

• *Remedy: Get feedback.* Feedback is the process by which the receiver "feeds back" to the sender what he thinks the sender meant. For example, if the sender says, "I need this information quickly," the receiver can ask, "Do you mean you want it by the end of the week?" The sender may say, "No, I want it before I leave the office tonight." Thus, feedback forestalls a potentially explosive situation in which one person expected something right away from another who thinks the information is due in a few days.

4. *Different general or technical vocabularies.* Most companies today have such diversified functions and departments as sales, production, contracting, research, budgeting, and so on. Each of these fields of specialization has developed specialized terminology known as jargon. Jargon is familiar to insiders and unintelligible to outsiders. When members or practitioners of various fields meet and try to communicate, they may "jargon" each other until no one knows what anyone else is saying. The conversation may sound vibrant and productive, but it's practically unintelligible to the participants.

An interesting—but disastrous—consequence of such meetings is that no one admits that he is not understanding the terminology being used. It's even harder for a subordinate to ask a supervisor what he means when the supervisor is jabbering away in abbreviations, acronyms, or jargon.

For example, such abbreviations as OSHA, FOB, FYI, and EEOC are useful when they save the effort of repeating their equivalents over and over again. But what about the receiver? Does he or she understand? Remember, most people are afraid to ask.

• *Remedy: Ask questions. Be empathetic.* Questions will solicit feedback. An effective communicator makes a habit of questioning any term, abbreviation, or acronym that he doesn't understand. This may take some nerve, but it is really an act of respect for the sender.

The sender, on the other hand, should use empathy. An empathetic communicator never uses an abbreviation unless he stops momentarily, puts himself in the position of the receiver, and makes sure that the abbreviation will be understood. If not, he will define it the first time he uses it.

5. *Lack of awareness of nonverbal symbols.* A substantial part of communication is nonverbal, and most of this nonverbal communication is *un*intentional and *un*conscious. These *un*intended messages, however, can have a devastating effect.

Nonverbal symbols comprise all ways, other than words, in which meanings are conveyed to others. Facial expressions, tone of voice, manner of dressing, behavior, gestures, silence, and all kinds of "body language" are forms of nonverbal communication.

For example, accounting supervisor John Stanley has just read a memo notifying him that one of his subordinates has made a major mistake in addition. He knows he will have to spend a good part of the day patching up the error. When he goes to speak with another subordinate, he speaks sharply and glares angrily at him. Unintentionally, he has communicated his anger to the *wrong* subordinate.

• *Remedy: Monitor yourself.* Any communicator can learn to monitor what he says or does and the effects produced. But it takes effort and a desire *not* to be misunderstood.

6. *One-way-only communication.* Many supervisors give one-way directions or advice and then move busily on to the next task—often leaving the subordinate baffled or frustrated.

Take the example of Joe Halpern, who told his secretary to "type this quickly" as he was walking out the door. She thought he wanted a rough draft. When he returned, he didn't have the final copy that he needed to bring to a meeting with him.

7. *Narrow, rigid viewpoints.* A group of communication researchers coined the term "allness" to reflect the tendency of some people to look at any situation from their own narrow point of view and assume that they "see" or "hear" *all* that is relevant or important. Usually, this kind of person blocks out anything that doesn't fit in with his view of reality.

Think of the supervisor in the shipping department, for example, who doesn't care what the product looks like as long he gets it on time. If the production manager has problems with uneven color or slightly unaligned parts, the shipping supervisor couldn't care less—he wants to maintain his record for prompt service. On the other hand, the production manager wants to maintain his record for high quality. Communication between the two is doomed from the start.

8. *The tendency to jump to conclusions.* People tend to jump to conclusions the moment they hear one fact or see a single act. For example, last week Mary Lewis's boss began a conversation with her by saying: "I've taken a good look at your salary level and, after careful consideration, . . ." Mary had already interrupted him mentally, without waiting for any more facts, with the thought that her present salary was being threatened. The result was that she interrupted him with a curt, snide remark before hearing what else he had to say.

• *Remedy: Suspend judgment.* Don't draw any conclusions until you have made a full effort to understand all the facts. If all the facts aren't immediately available, suspend judgment until all the results are in.

9. *Distractions.* Sometimes the cause of communication breakdown is simply distraction. Time pressure may force attention away from what is being communicated; the physical environment may be threatening or uncomfortable; there may be too much noise; it may be Friday afternoon before a Monday holiday; the receiver or sender may be having personal problems.

• *Remedy: Acknowledge the distraction.* Empathy leads the able communicator to acknowledge—rather than to ignore—the distractions and, thus, deal with them in a common-sense way. The empathetic communicator asks questions or uses feedback to find out whether distraction is ruining the communication attempt. If it is, he removes the distraction or plans to continue the communication another time.

(Reprinted from SUPERVISORY MANAGEMENT, May 1973)

Susan Sinclair

Transactional Analysis—or "What do you mean, my report was late?"

RECENTLY, a supervisor told me: "When I became a supervisor, I thought all my problems were going to be mechanical. But they aren't. The majority of my problems are people problems."

Transactional analysis (TA) is one approach that this supervisor could use to solve his people problems. Through transactional analysis, a supervisor can learn to understand his subordinates' behavior and open up lines of communication that have previously been closed.

Simply defined, transactional analysis is an approach to understanding human behavior based on how people relate to each other—that is, how they interact. The *analysis* involved is undertaken by studying the "transactions" between people—by tracing the way in which a transaction is shaped by the particular ego state of each person. There are three possible ego states that determine behavior—Parent, Adult, and Child—and they are largely programmed on the basis of prior experiences and feelings. As with most theories about ways to change behavior, transactional analysis presumes that aware-

Manager, Flight Service, Regional Training, Pan American World Airways

83

ness of their ego states by the people involved in a transaction can help them understand and thereafter change their behavior.

Eric Berne, the originator of transactional analysis, first recognized the value of viewing transactions between people in terms of whether their ego states at the time were based on their Child, Parent, or Adult programming. For Berne, the Parent is a taught concept of life learned by each of us before the age of five—concepts built on the external experiences, admonitions, feelings, and behavior that were impressed on us when we could only accept without question or qualification. The Child, on the other hand, is the internal response we make up to about the age of five to what we see and hear; it is our feelings and understandings of our experiences, mostly feelings. Lastly, the Adult is the ego state that emerges as we begin to explore the world and to see and hear and feel a variety of experiences that give us a basis for new ideas that may challenge both the admonitions of our Parent state and the unrefined feelings of our Child. Although each of us typically will live most of life in one of these ego states, we often adopt a different state in critical or emotional relationships or to accomplish a planned end. In any case, we are all capable of going from one ego state to another almost instantaneously if something in our situation happens to press the right button in our programming.

Life script

A response pattern learned in childhood that continues into his maturity is part of a person's "life script." Much like a theatrical script, the "life script" determines most of a person's life patterns—complete with cast of characters, dialogue, acts, themes, and plots. Many people are unaware of what their life scripts are—yet they compulsively act them out in their everyday behavior.

If, for example, a parent treats a child as if he were unlovable, the child may grow up to be an adult who perpetually feels unlovable. He may feel (unconsciously) that the only way he can be loved is by acting like a parent—since his parents didn't seem to like children very much. Or the reverse may happen: The child may end up responding to most situations as a child—even when he is far past his teens.

Our life scripts have been rather securely programmed into us—and few people can change without some kind of therapy or intensive introspection. Only then can they begin to change their life scripts and start responding in the present rather than the past.

Supervisors, of course, are not therapists—but they can use trans-actional-analysis techniques to motivate subordinates and establish better communication with them. How? By understanding what life scripts or patterns both they and their subordinates have adopted. Once they can see the pattern, they can begin to have some control over their responses or ego states involved in relating with subordinates. This ability to control—at least in part—his responses to a subordinate can help the supervisor motivate employees as well as break any counterproductive patterns that have been set up between them.

What's my line?

As mentioned above, in TA lingo, the sets of programming or ego states that influence each of our transactions are called Parent, Adult, and Child—and are symbolized by the letters P, A, and C, with each letter circled:

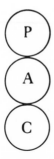

The particular ego state that a person assumes—consciously or unconsciously—in relation to another person will have a decided impact on his or her attitude and subsequent behavior. Consider the following dialogue between supervisor and subordinate. At its culmination, the supervisor is left with a clear need to influence his subordinate to take proper action. The response he makes will be crucial in achieving this goal.

Supervisor: "Bill, call Jackson Iron Works and try to close that order."

Salesman: "I've tried twice, and both times they said they hadn't made up their minds yet."

Supervisor: "Well, call again. If we wait too long, we'll lose the order."
Salesman: "I've tried. Why don't you do it?"

What kind of response will be the most effective for the supervisor in this situation? Take a look at the following alternatives, each of which represents a different kind of attitude or ego state.

"What do you think you're getting paid for?" (This represents the Parent ego state.)

"Bill, I could do it, but since you've been working on the Jackson account for two months, you'd probably have a better chance of closing the deal." (This represents the Adult ego state.)

"Listen, you guys think I can do your work as well as my work. I've got problems of my own, you know." (This represents the Child ego state.)

Parent

The Parent ego state represents all the attitudes and behaviors that we have copied from our parents and others who served as parent figures as we were growing up—for example, teachers, brothers and sisters, and grandparents. Outward behavior toward others expressed from this ego state can be prejudicial, critical, or nurturing. Our feelings about politics, religion, business ethics, goals, and social courtesies usually come from the Parent ego state, since it has been the vehicle for transmitting culture from generation to generation. The list below will give you an idea of some of the verbal and nonverbal behavioral clues that identify the Parent ego state.

VERBAL CLUES	NONVERBAL CLUES
always, never, remember, stupid, shocking, absurd, ridiculous, disgusting, asinine; if I were you; as long as you live (or) work in this department; unthinking, judgmental reactions of all types; *poor thing; honey; dear.*	pointing a finger accusingly; shaking your head; wringing your hands; tapping your foot; standing or sitting with arms folded; pursing your lips; sighing; snorting impatiently; patting a person on the head or shoulder; making consoling sounds; holding and rocking.

Adult

The Adult ego state, which has nothing to do with age, is related to the person's ability to size up reality, to analyze the odds, and to act accordingly. A person who communicates from this ego state has no predetermined feelings—unlike the person who communicates from the Parent or Child state. However, after checking out the situation, he might *choose* to respond in the Parent or the Child state—if either were more appropriate.

Here are some clues for identifying the Adult ego state:

VERBAL CLUES

why, what, when, where, how; alternatives; restating what the other person has said in order to check understanding.

NONVERBAL CLUES

concerned, interested appearance; erect posture; lively facial expressions; appropriate responses to what others are saying.

Child

The Child ego state includes all the impulses that come naturally to a child. When a person is in the Child ego state, he is not necessarily being childish. Instead, he is acting and feeling as he did when he was a child. This state encompasses the creative, self-centered, rebellious, affectionate, fun-loving nature and curiosity that are in each of us. Whenever you have the urge to touch despite a sign warning, "Do Not Touch," you are aware of your Child. The following list gives clues to the presence of your Child ego state:

VERBAL CLUES

I don't care, I hope, I want, I wish, baby talk, *look at mine, now, wow, gee whiz, I'm scared, mine's bigger and better than yours* (also called *"keeping up with the Jones's"*), backbiting when another person has left the room.

NONVERBAL CLUES

tears, pouting, temper tantrums, high-pitched, whining voice, no answer, downcast eyes, nose thumbing, giggling, squirming, teasing, taunting, needling.

If you're speaking with someone and you can't figure out which ego state he is in, the rule of thumb is to rely on nonverbal clues. The supervisor, for example, who makes an appointment with a subordinate in order to commend him for a job well done will sound insincere if he spends most of his time shuffling papers or if he doesn't look directly at the subordinate when he is speaking to him.

Communication

Since no one communicates in a vacuum, it's important to analyze these three ego states as they relate to transactions between two or more people. The following diagrams will help you analyze most transactions. The sender (or stimulus) is always on the left and the respondent (or response) is always on the right. Follow the arrows from left to right, then from right to left in order to get the flow of the transaction. There are three basic types of transactions: (1) complementary (see p. 89), (2) crossed (see p. 90), and (3) ulterior (see p. 91).

Direction

A basic understanding of how ego states work during transactions may help you pinpoint and analyze problems that come up in your interactions with subordinates.

Let's say, for example, that after you have counseled a subordinate, she bursts into tears in order to avoid any further confrontation. Or consider the case of the female supervisor who gets this response from a male subordinate: "Do you realize how long I've been with this company, young lady?"

In situations like these, it's best for the supervisor to stay in the Adult ego state if he or she wants to achieve some kind of positive behavioral response or change from a subordinate. A concerned, interested appearance and the use of such words as *why, what, where, when, who,* and *how* are helpful. Other techniques: listing alternatives or restating what the other person said in order to make sure that you understood him correctly. But make sure the worker doesn't get the idea that you are mocking him when you restate what he has said.

In certain situations, staying in the Adult ego state may be quite difficult. Your strongest urge may be to slip into the critical Parent and, *whammo,* let him have it. If you can stick with the Adult, however, the person with whom you are dealing will eventually come around and listen to what you have to say.

COMPLEMENTARY TRANSACTION

In a complementary transaction, the lines of communication are parallel and, therefore, the conversation can go on indefinitely. In this type of transaction, the sender can usually predict the response he will get. Below are examples of a complementary parent/parent transaction and a complementary child/nurturing parent transaction.

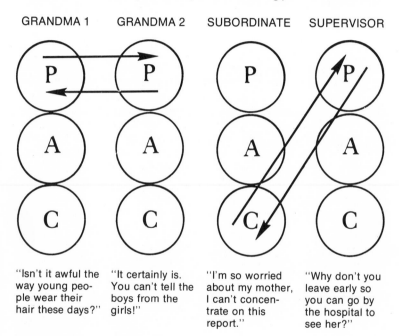

GRANDMA 1	GRANDMA 2	SUBORDINATE	SUPERVISOR
"Isn't it awful the way young people wear their hair these days?"	"It certainly is. You can't tell the boys from the girls!"	"I'm so worried about my mother, I can't concentrate on this report."	"Why don't you leave early so you can go by the hospital to see her?"

Stroking

A basic behavior in transactions is stroking. A supervisor can use this technique in his interactions with subordinates in order to motivate, reward, or reprimand them. Strokes are any signs of recognition or touch—whether they are negative or positive. They can be given in the form of a compliment, an actual physical touch, or such nonverbal recognition as a smile, a nod, or a wink. In other words, any act that says "I know you're there" is a stroke. Strokes that make us feel bad are called discounts—e.g., ignoring or isolating someone. The person who gives out that kind of discount is actually treating an adult as if he were a child.

According to all the studies that have been done—not only with animals, but also with human beings—positive stroking is necessary for healthy survival. In a study conducted at a European orphanage a

---

CROSSED TRANSACTION

In a crossed transaction, the sender often receives a response that he does not expect. When the lines of communication cross, communication stops.

In the first transaction below, for example, Worker 1 addresses Worker 2 as an adult, but Worker 2 responds as a child. In the second transaction, Husband acts like a parent who is talking to a child. But Wife does not respond as a child. She, too, acts like a parent. It's easy to see how lines of communication get tangled.

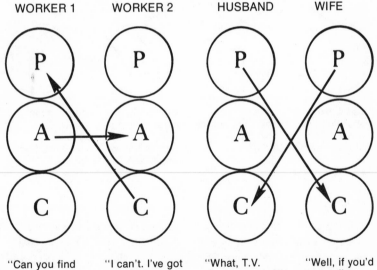

WORKER 1   WORKER 2   HUSBAND   WIFE

"Can you find any more order forms? I'm just about out."

"I can't. I've got 13 million other things to do first."

"What, T.V. dinners again?"

"Well, if you'd ever tell me when you're coming home, you'd get a decent meal!"

ULTERIOR TRANSACTION

An ulterior transaction is always more complex than either a complementary or a crossed transaction because it involves more than
two ego states for each person simultaneously. Often, as illustrated
below, what appears to be an adult-adult communication may
underneath be an adult-child or a child-child communication.

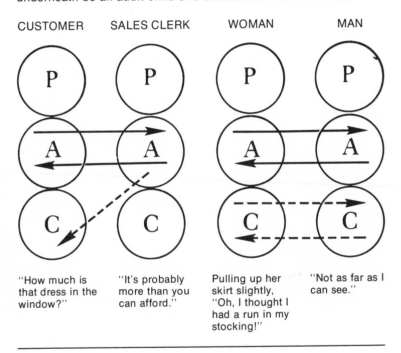

CUSTOMER	SALES CLERK	WOMAN	MAN

"How much is that dress in the window?"

"It's probably more than you can afford."

Pulling up her skirt slightly, "Oh, I thought I had a run in my stocking!"

"Not as far as I can see."

number of years ago, half of the babies were given tender, loving care
(TLC) by the workers at the orphanage. The other half were ignored
and picked up only for diaper changing and feeding. At the end of the
study, the babies who had been given TLC were happy, healthy, and
seemingly well adjusted. Several of the deprived ones had died, and
many of the others showed signs of both mental and physical retarda-
tion. These results show that strokes involve more than just being nice
to people. They are a way to help human beings meet their needs for
physical and mental growth.

Stroking can sometimes be as reinforcing as pay. A well-paid research analyst, for example, was very productive for the first six to eight months on the job. But over the next few months, his work started to slide in quality and quantity. His supervisor, who had recently attended a transactional analysis seminar, decided to use the techniques to figure out where the problem was.

He noticed that the researcher spent a great deal of time in the lounge where workers went to get their coffee on coffee breaks. Unlike most of the other workers, the researcher worked alone in his laboratory and seldom had any visitors. From that time on, the supervisor tried to drop by the lab at least twice a day—sometimes for no other reason than to say *hello*. Within a few weeks, the long coffee breaks ended and the researcher's productivity returned to its previously high level.

When someone gives positive recognition, it is much better to give that recognition without any conditions attached to it. In other words, stroking for being is far superior to stroking for doing. Why? It's like the mother who tells her child, ''I love you when you behave,'' instead of, ''I love you.''

You can use your Adult understanding of your subordinates' need for stroking by noticing them, initiating some kind of communication with them, and letting them know that their work is important to the organization as a whole. The supervisor who communicates as a critical Parent (''Do your work!'') or critical Adult (''I don't care what you feel; I'm interested only in facts!'') will rarely evoke loyalty or enthusiasm from his subordinates. The most effective stroking is usually given by the nurturing parent (''Is there something wrong?'').

Put it all together

You can use your knowledge of transactional analysis to try to understand and motivate your subordinates. In some cases, you may want to give unconditional strokes and act as a nurturing Parent. In other cases, you may want to counter a worker's Child with a strongly Adult approach. Or you may want to cajole or subtly manipulate a worker for his or her own good. In that case, you may have to communicate from your Child ego state.

Sara Pearson, for example, used this technique with Natalie Smith, a sewing operator at a lingerie plant. Natalie was petrified of the new sewing machine that had just been installed—but she didn't want to tell Sara. Instead of yelling at her or admonishing her publicly for not turning out more work, Sara slipped into a Child role and called Natalie over. "Oh, Natalie, don't tell anyone, but this new machine is a bit much for me. Do you think you could show me the way to work it?"

After showing her boss how she used the machine, Natalie gained more confidence and realized that the new machine actually made her work easier. She also felt proud that she could explain something to her supervisor. Sara's understanding of the dynamics of transactional analysis helped her solve a near crisis with a subordinate.

(Reprinted from SUPERVISORY MANAGEMENT, October 1973)

Jack J. Holder

The Uncommunicators

"I wish Pete would let me get back to work," thought chief engineer Terry Clark. "Every afternoon, he comes into my office and gives me a full report of what happened in the drafting department during the day. Sparing no details, he ticks off—one by one—the tasks he has accomplished, the problems he has had with subordinates, and the conversations he has had with production—and here he goes again. Whew!"

Terry started straightening his desk and making motions that signaled his desire to get to work—but Pete continued his ceaseless monologue. Finally, Terry just got up and mumbled something about having to see about the plans for the new minicomputer.

Simply stated, Pete the Pest (as his supervisor was beginning to think of him) was an overcommunicator. He communicated so much that everything he said to Terry carried the same weight. Terry never knew what Pete considered *pressing* and what he considered *trivial*. Pete expected Terry to sift through the information. But after a while, Terry got tired of having to do all the work. Terry believed in "management by exception"—and with Peter there were no exceptions.

Pete the Pest had a communication difficulty: He reported everything and, as a result, ended up communicating nothing. Furthermore, he was almost oblivious to nonverbal cues from his boss.

Assistant Vice-President, Yellow Freight System, Inc.

Do you recognize Pete in any of your co-workers or subordinates? Supervisors with a communication problem can severely hamper work flow and productivity in their units because their subordinates and superiors literally do not know what is going on. In Pete's case, his attitude actually prevented his superior from getting his own work done. In other cases, subordinates may be getting the wrong messages from their supervisors—or no message at all.

Pete is only one example of a supervisor with a communication problem. Following is a sampling of a few more. Do you recognize any of your subordinates or peers? Do you see yourself?

Elrod the Unready. When Elrod Jones called a staff meeting in order to explain a new procedure for dye cutting, he sent out a badly written memo. Then he started the meeting with a poorly worded statement about the process, which he had not taken the time to understand himself. The discussion during the meeting was imprecise, loosely structured, and rambling. When the meeting was finally over, his subordinates—obviously worried and concerned about the new process—reluctantly went back to their machines. They still didn't understand the new process, but they knew enough about it to be apprehensive.

When a supervisor doesn't carefully prepare his memos or organize his meetings so that they run smoothly and productively, the result can be confusion, misunderstanding and, ultimately, lower profits for the company.

Words, like rockets on their way to the moon, have a far better chance of hitting their target and accomplishing their objectives if they are carefully aimed before launching. A supervisor who doesn't choose his words carefully and plan what he is going to say before speaking may be surprised to find out that even though *he* knows what he means, his subordinates are still in the dark or may have six different interpretations of what they think he means.

Martha the Memomaniac. Martha first started having a communication problem about six years ago when she wrote her first memo. Since then, she has papered her entire department with memos until her subordinates, superiors, and peers have gotten the impression that she would rather write memos than talk. Of course, memos are useful—particularly when you are trying to communicate with many people at one time or when you want to get something down on paper for future reference. But there is a limit. The situation became unbearable when Martha started sending out memos in which she would openly criticize a subordinate. One of her subordinates began to tremble at the sight of Martha's white "billets-doux." Another would sandwich them between scads of paper in his in-box and let them languish before reading them.

Martha may be afraid to communicate with her subordinates or superiors face to face or she may not know how to express herself orally. Whatever the reason, her memos are an imprecise form of communication. Because she relies on the written word in commanding and directing her subordinates, she is never able to explore with a subordinate the nuances of the communication and answer any questions he may have.

Although it may take more time and may cost more money—in the beginning—to talk, rather than write, the payoff is better communication, increased understanding, and greater efficiency. If *you* have to send a memo, use it to confirm a conversational exchange. But get the job done with back-and-forth talks.

George the Genius. George Chapin went right from a fine eastern prep school to a well-known college—though he didn't graduate. Something about what Miss Peregrine said in English X101 must have stuck in his mind, because all his memos sounded like the following:

> We will determine the potential benefits to be derived from implementation of an improved system in broad terms and assign priorities for proceeding with the installation of the individual project areas, based upon our evaluation of the advantages to be obtained versus the time and cost required for implementation and operation of the new application.

Would you believe that what he really wanted to say was: Are you going to help us increase the production of nuts and bolts?

Communicators like George actually impede communication when they could use their abilities to improve it. It takes effort and perseverence to learn to express oneself clearly and precisely. Yet George chose the easy way out: to write down whatever came into his mind without carefully assessing whether his words were unambiguous or his meaning a mystery to anyone except George.

Part of George's problem is that he writes abstractly, requiring the reader to visualize the concepts he is trying to convey rather than attempting to let the words speak for themselves. In a sense, George is withholding meaning from the reader by refusing to go out of his way to make things understandable—and this snobbery is ruining production in his department.

Selma the Silent. Selma was not ordinarily a quiet person—except when it came to her job. Selma used silence the way some people use words—to communicate her attitudes and opinions. When she disagreed with a superior, she would delay answering his or her memo. Her boss hardly knew what was going on in Selma's department because she kept him informed about only the things he already knew about. Her subordinates never knew where they stood with Selma because she never gave them any feedback—negative or positive. When she was asked to answer a specific question, she would avoid saying anything direct so that the questioner would have to pick the answer out of the air. This is no easy trick when the question concerns the company policy on vacations for employees who had been with the company over three years.

Selma was an *under*communicator who used silence as a strategy to convey her meaning. But often her meaning was misunderstood. Her boss began to wonder whether there wasn't something wrong in Selma's department. Why had she waited so long to send in the monthly budget? Why hadn't she told him about Jackie Ingrassia's transfer to special projects? Was there something that Selma was trying to hide?

Selma's *under*communication was as detrimental to her department as was Pete's *over*communication. But unlike Pete's staff, her subordinates didn't know how they were doing and, as a result, turnover in her unit was high. Subordinates found it difficult to function in an ambiguous atmosphere where the only time they got any criticism was during their yearly performance review. Some of them didn't remain long enough to be reviewed anyway. The ones who remained were self-motivated but never developed to their fullest potential. How could they when they never knew where they should improve and when they were performing adequately?

Arnold the Arrogant. Everyone knows an Arnold, and some are even unlucky enough to work with one. Arnold does not communicate; he legislates. When Arnold speaks, everyone around him must listen reverently, for Arnold speaks the truth (according to Arnold, that is). When one of his subordinates speaks to Arnold, there is

FAT TALK
By Russell Baker

Americans don't like plain talk anymore. Nowadays they like fat talk. Show them a lean, plain word that cuts to the bone and watch them lard it with thick greasy syllables front and back until it wheezes and gasps for breath as it comes lumbering down upon some poor threadbare sentence like a sack of iron on a swayback horse.

"Facilitate" is typical of the case. A generation ago only sissies and bureaucrats would have said "facilitate" in public. Nowadays we are a nation of "facilitate" utterers.

"Facilitate" is nothing more than a gout-ridden, overstuffed "ease." Why has "ease" fallen into disuse among us? It is a lovely little bright snake of a word that comes hissing quietly off the tongue and carries us on, without fuss and French horns, to the object that is being eased.

This is English at its very best. Easing is not one of the great events of life; it does not call for Beethoven; it is not an idea to get drunk on, to wallow in, to encase in multiple oleaginous syllabification until it becomes a pompous ass of a word like "facilitate."

There is a radio disk jocky who cannot bring himself to say that the temperature at the studio is "now" 45 degrees but must fatten it up, extend it, make more of it, score it for kettle drums—by declaring that the temperature at the studio is "currently" 45 degrees and often, carried into illiteracy in his passion for fat talk, "presently" 45 degrees.

Newspapers seem to be the father and mother of fat. The bombing is never the stark, dramatic "intense," but always the drawled, overweight "intensive." Presidents are rarely allowed to "say" the weather is improving; the papers have them "declare" it, "state" it, "issue a challenge for the Weather Bureau to deny" it.

Why do we like our words so fat but our women so skinny?

*—Condensed from The New York Times (January 4, 1973), © 1973
by The New York Times Company.*

a moment of silence in which Arnold nods his head, feigning interest; then he impatiently interrupts with: "Why I told you all that before, John. You know my theory about interpersonal interaction between peers of the same ethnic background in an industrial, organizational setting. Yes, yes, of course, you feel that way. . . ."

The trouble with Arnold is that often his subordinates, peers, and superiors don't feel the way he tells them to. They are human beings and, consequently, they resist being categorized or stereotyped in one of Arnold's neatly packed little boxes. This makes no difference to Arnold, however. He blithely goes along interpreting reality to suit his own purposes.

Arnold is a true *un*communicator because he pays no attention to what anyone says or feels—unless it relates directly to him or something he believes. For this reason, Arnold has never gotten very far in his company. While he is an excellent systems analyst, his attitude has destroyed morale in his department. His subordinates can be seen nodding blandly at everything Arnold says. But somehow, management talent always seems to show up in the other supervisors' departments.

When Arnold's supervisor tried to tell him about his inability to listen with an open mind, Arnold got extremely angry and said, "I've been around a lot longer than you, young man. When you know as much about life as I do, then you can tell me about human relations. I'm devoted to my subordinates, and I hold their best interests at heart. How dare you tell me that I lack communication skills? Ask them if they understand me!"

Tony the Telephoner. Tony likes to conduct all his business on the telephone. Luckily for him, he's a salesman and his job requires that a certain amount of his time be spent on the telephone. "Hello, Jack . . ." "Hello, Harry . . ." "Hello, Fred . . . ," Tony can be heard yelling into the telephone receiver all day long. Tony even calls his subordinates: "Hello, Mary, where's my report for the sales meeting?" "Max, where's the piece goods?"

Unfortunately, deals cannot always be closed on the telephone—nor can subordinates be appraised that way, or budgets submitted. When Tony has to address a sales meeting, he gets a pained expression on his face, and his right hand seems to twitch at his side. Could it be reaching for the telephone?

Supervisors like Tony have a significant communication problem because they use the telephone as a crutch on which to lean all their insecurities. They do not try to learn to communicate in person with co-workers, subordinates, and superiors because it's easier for them to relate to the impersonality of the telephone. Telephones are an essential part of modern management in this technological age, but they cannot yet communicate the varied facial expressions, attitudes, emotional overtones, or subtle, nonverbal cues of a face-to-face conversation. A perceptive supervisor can usually look at a subordinate and know that something is wrong. This is particularly important when the supervisor is explaining a procedure or task that the subordinate must fully understand in order to execute it. How will the supervisor know whether the subordinate understands him if he gives his instructions over the telephone?

Tom the Untimely. Tom believes that there is no time like the present, so whenever the urge hits him, he communicates. This gets Tom into all kinds of trouble since timing is a subtle communication skill that must be used as carefully as words.

Tom bursts into his boss's office the moment something happens that he thinks he should report. It doesn't matter to him that the director of marketing is standing by the door. One time, the director of marketing *was* just walking out the door when Tom burst in with the news that his unit had goofed on the monthly figures and were over budget by $2,000. Tom's supervisor turned red with embarrassment—particularly since he had just assured the director of marketing that everything was fine in their department. It turned out that Tom had made a serious multiplication error—but not as serious as what he had done to his boss.

Tom had another "untimely" habit. He would often give subordinates directions as they were leaving on a Friday night. It wasn't that he was trying to be mean. He was just completely unaware of other people's feelings or of external events. Although Tom had no trouble with words and was well known for his impeccable memos, he had a hard time knowing when to open or close his mouth.

Timing is essential to good communication because the right message at the wrong time may carry an entirely different meaning than the one intended. Telling a subordinate that he is going to be transferred on the day he comes back to work from vacation is as detrimental to staff productivity as telling a subordinate that you have decided to promote him when he is standing within earshot of two of his coworkers.

Uncommunicators are not unreachable. Remember that if you have one in your department or if you are one yourself, awareness is the key to good communication ability. Develop a person's insight into the ways in which he interacts with others and chances are that he will modify his behavior to become more effective in his job. Communication is a skill that can be learned, just like computation or coordination. Fortunately, few people are as extreme as Martha, Tom, Arnold, Tony, Pete, George, and Selma—but there might be a little of them in all of us.

(Reprinted from SUPERVISORY MANAGEMENT, July 1973)

Bernard B. Beegle

The Message That Is Sent Without Words

COMMUNICATION is like an iceberg—only a small part of it lies above the surface. The part that does could be termed *verbal communication:* the exchange of information in speech or writing. Lying just below the water level is *nonverbal communication:* the exchange of information through subtle visual signs such as gestures or mannerisms.

Much of the literature on communication deals only with the peak of the iceberg, the verbal communication. Only recently has the language of nonverbal communication gained widespread attention. Fluency in this language is vital to effective supervision. The supervisor who responds appropriately to the meaning of a shrug of the shoulders, a sigh, or a moment of silence has a better basis of understanding with his subordinates and is in a better position to gain their cooperation.

Perhaps the major problem in nonverbal communication, however, is that it tends to go unnoticed—or is dismissed as trivial. "I'm no mind reader," says the person who wants to get himself off the hook for not solving a subordinate's problem. "If Arthur doesn't *tell* me what's bothering him, how am I supposed to know?" Sometimes non-

Supervisor of Industrial Engineering, Sperry Rand Corporation

verbal communications are indeed noticed—but the problems involved are given mere lip service, as the following example illustrates.

Mabel, a file clerk, always gave her supervisor a cordial "Good morning" as he entered the department each day. However, for the past two days, she had stopped greeting him informally and there seemed to be a change in her behavior. She was less talkative and less pleasant; she kept her attention fixed to paperwork on her desk.

On the third day, the supervisor called Mabel into his office and got her to explain what was the matter. The upshot of the conversation was that the supervisor asked Mabel to put her grievance into writing and give him a memo on the subject. "Then I'll be able to do something about it," he said. However, Mabel never did put the complaint into writing, nor did the supervisor encourage her further to do so. From the supervisor's point of view, the problem was solved because "he had done his part." No one could accuse him of not caring.

Responsibility for action

Young employees, especially, would be likely to call the supervisor's action in this case a *cop-out*—that is, a failure to handle the problem in a direct manner. If the complaint was legitimate, the supervisor should have made sure the memo was written; if the employee was unable or unwilling to write the memo herself, the supervisor should have found out why and provided assistance or sought another solution. If, on the other hand, he considered the complaint unfounded, he would have been wiser to tell the subordinate this. By doing so, he might have run the risk of her immediate displeasure, but their communication would at least have been on the up and up. As it is, the supervisor will surely have further problems with this particular file clerk.

Barometer of morale

Subtle changes in attitudes and morale can be expressed in many ways. Let us look at another example. A supervisor walking through his department noticed that several employees at one work station gave him a quick, cold glance and then turned abruptly away. These employees were communicating nonverbally—through gestures and mannerisms—hoping the supervisor would take time to talk to them.

At this point, the supervisor had a choice. He could have refused to acknowledge the communication—rationalizing that nothing was communicated because no words were spoken. Or he could have responded to their "message" by pausing at the work station to give them time to say what was the matter or—if this was not forthcoming—to make his own tactful inquiries.

Of course, phrasing a tactful question is an art in itself—the words and the tone of voice you use strongly determine the frankness of the answer you get. Furthermore, communication with each employee must be tailored—the way you say something to Ralph might not work with Joe, and so on.

The important point is that nonverbal communication is a frequently used and significant way for employees to express what's on their minds. Indeed, it is sometimes the only way that employees know how to say, "Boss, something is really bothering me. I'd like to talk to you about it."

It's in the supervisor's own interest to *observe* how his subordinates communicate through gestures and mannerisms and to *acknowledge* these signs as legitimate messages that demand attention. When employees communicate nonverbally, they are signaling you to get involved. They are asking you to take the initiative to talk to them, to find out if problems exist, and to take action to solve them quickly. Your responsiveness to nonverbal communication shows the extent of your interest in your subordinates—and they will respond accordingly.

(Reprinted from SUPERVISORY MANAGEMENT, February 1971)

Jack H. Grossman

Are Your Messages Provoking Conflict?

A BREAKDOWN in communication is the beginning of many human relations conflicts. Somewhere along the line, the sender's message becomes warped and the receiver reacts to the unintended distortion. When, for example, you ask your secretary, "Is the XYZ report finished yet?" you simply want information—but she thinks you're chiding her for not having the report ready and becomes defensive.

Opportunities for conflict exist in all boss-subordinate relationships. A says so-and-so and B thinks he means such-and-such, which B resents; therefore, B says so-and-so, which A takes to mean thus-and-such and also resents; whereupon A says so-and-so, which makes B a little hotter; and so on and on. Keeping the peace depends heavily on the supervisor's ability (to quote Eric Webster, a British management expert) to "keep the mess out of the message."

Causing the mess, of course, are all the habits and mental quirks that make people human: We jump to conclusions, we go out of our way to avoid threats that don't exist, we fall victim to biases, we mistrust others without cause. This is the mine field that any message must cross on its way to being heard, understood, and believed.

Assistant Professor of Management, College of Commerce, DePaul University

Count to ten first

The more vague a statement, the greater its chance of being misunderstood. Hence, it always pays to make your messages, whether written or spoken, adequately informative. That is, if you ask a question simply to get information, make sure the other person knows your motive so that he won't think, for example, that you're rebuking him.

Suppose, however, that the XYZ report is already a day late. You want to know why and you want your secretary to know you're dissatisfied with the delay. In an angry tone, you say the first thing that comes to mind: "Why isn't the XYZ report finished?" She fires back angrily with an excuse because your approach automatically put her on the defensive.

A more precise and constructive way to get your message across is to say: "I expected the report by this time; when can I have it?" This message is not a direct attack. Rather, it calls her attention to the standard set for the task and lets her know how you feel without causing any hard feelings. At the same time, it generates the information—and the cooperation—you really want.

The same rules hold when you're the message receiver or, as in the case of the following employee, the nonmessage receiver. The employee had been on his first job for about 17 months, and it had been some time since he had received a salary increase. As he weighed the pros and cons of approaching his boss, he thought to himself, "If I asked him, chances are he'd turn me down. Why would he turn me down? If that's all he thinks of me, I'd better look for another job." With this, he marched into his boss's office and announced, "I quit!"

The boss, of course, was shocked at his subordinate's seemingly irrational behavior and insisted on knowing its cause. "Why didn't you ask me about a raise?" he said after hearing the story. "Your appraisal is due next week, and I had already planned to put you in for one!"

Don't jump to conclusions

Incidents like this are not uncommon. In the face of what we believe is a threat to our ego, we try to second-guess the other person, seeing in him motives and attitudes that he may not have, simply to protect ourselves from possible embarrassment. But when we react to a threat that doesn't exist, or act on an assumption that is erroneous, we blind ourselves to the truth, often hurting ourselves and others in the process.

Therefore, when you're unsure of a speaker's intent, don't jump to the conclusion that you're being reprimanded. If your boss asks you, "Is the XYZ report ready yet?" interpret his statement not as a criticism but as a simple request for information. Or, if talk has gone far beyond that stage and you find yourself the object of a tirade, keep your boss's comments in perspective. You might ask yourself, "Is it me, or did I approach him at the wrong time?" Remember that all of us have days in which things go wrong. A bad start in the morning can ruin an entire day, causing us to fly off the handle regardless of what is said or who says it.

Accuracy is the basis for all effective communication, and using precisely worded statements is the first step toward being understood. But believed? That's another matter. The boss who tells a subordinate that he's doing a "fine job" on Monday, but criticizes him for "always being careless" on Tuesday is obviously not building a reputation for credibility.

Words, after all, are just labels for objects and actions. To the extent that your behavior is consistent with your words, subordinates will trust what you say. But permit one too many inconsistencies—a compliment you don't really mean, a promise you've no intention of keeping—and subordinates will start being suspicious of everything you say.

This is why words alone are not enough to motivate people or even to keep harmony in the department. You have to develop ways to back up what you say—for example, a simple smile, an especially complimentary sentence in an appraisal, or delegation of a special project.

Actions speak louder . . .

It works the other way, too, of course. When you're displeased with a subordinate's performance, you have to say so, or your silence will be interpreted as approval. One sales manager, for example, who fashioned himself as a "nice guy," was loath to jeopardize that image by criticizing a salesman's poor performance.

"How do you handle such salesmen?" he was asked.

"I just let them hang themselves," he said.

The supervisor's unspoken displeasure is bound to be reflected in other areas of his relationship with that subordinate. His attitude will make the subordinate feel uncomfortable enough to test his boss's reactions in the hope of finding out what he really thinks. All the while, the supervisor's dissatisfaction will fester, creating a climate rife with distrust.

The only solution is to confront the subordinate with the facts of his performance. You can do so without offending him if you observe the following rules:

• Have clearly publicized standards for employee performance. When a subordinate fails to meet those standards, show him exactly what he has failed to do by objectively comparing his performance to the standards.

• Voice your displeasure as soon as you realize that standards are not being met. Keeping quiet and stewing about the situation will make you overreact when you finally do explode.

• Listen to the employee's point of view. Remember that most people have an emotional investment in their ideas. If you think there's a risk that you'll disparage their thinking, they won't level with you. You must assure them that their ideas will be understood, respected, and evaluated on their merits.

How to handle your biases

The commitment of straightforward communication is not easy to keep, for no one has complete control of his basic attitude toward life and people. We tend to feel closer to people who are similar to us and to mistrust anyone whose values differ greatly from our own.

Suppose, for example, that an employee who wants an advance on his salary approaches a supervisor who believes that people should budget their money from one pay period to another. Chances are that the supervisor will disapprove of such a request and probably of the employee as well. That is, judgments of behavior generally lead to judgments of people. A person who performs more slowly than others is thought to be lazy; a person who makes an arithmetical error is deemed careless; someone who wears flashy clothes is viewed as cheap.

Obviously, you won't change your values unless you have some compelling reason to do so—and even then it's difficult. But you can improve your communication with people who don't share your values by asking these questions:

- Am I judging this person as a unique individual rather than as a member of a group?
- Do I have my facts straight about the person's performance?
- Do his values really threaten mine or not?
- Am I reacting to his beliefs because of their potential harm to me or simply because they are alien to me?

Answers to these questions will help you be more objective in your communication, a major step toward building a relationship of mutual trust with employees.

Some guidelines

However, you must weigh each situation and be sufficiently flexible to adjust your communication to the person. To achieve more harmonious interpersonal relations, try the following suggestions:

1. Always try to specify the purpose of your communication; leave as little as possible to the listener's imagination.

2. Always verify that you have correctly understood the messages you receive. You might lead in by saying, "If I understood what you said, you meant. . . ."

3. Before taking any action, have your facts straight and check out your assumptions. If it's not feasible to obtain the necessary facts at that moment, let the other person know that your remarks are based on assumptions and leave the door open for discussion.

4. Make your expectations known. Let subordinates know the standards against which you will measure their performance.

5. Always direct criticism at the act, not at the person. And always provide him with directions for improving.

6. Always support your words with action, and don't promise anything you can't back up.

7. Phrase your messages to encourage positive action rather than defensive behavior. Instead of saying, "You didn't do . . . ," say "I need . . . so that I can get my work done."

8. Listen to what your subordinates say. Don't be so intent on getting your point across that you don't hear the other person's side of the story.

(Reprinted from SUPERVISORY MANAGEMENT, November 1970)

Lewis R. Benton

When Your Only Answer Is "No"

"YOU KNOW what I need?" one manager asked another over a morning cup of coffee. "I need a good way to say 'No' so that it sounds like 'Yes.' Yesterday one of my clerks asked me if she could leave two hours early, because some furniture was being delivered to her apartment and she had to be there to let the men in. I told her right away that it was out of the question because of the rush order we had to get out. You know what she did? She started to cry. And she hasn't said two words to me since. She's making me feel like a real monster."

There are times when a manager has to say "No." Not every request from a subordinate can be granted; it may be unreasonable, against company policy, impractical, or—as in this situation—untimely. But there's a strong temptation for the manager to say "Yes" and avoid unpleasantness. He wants to be thought of as a good boss, he wants to be liked, he wants satisfied subordinates.

When you buy popularity through easy acquiescence, however, the price can be high. If this manager had acceded to his clerk's request to leave early, he would have kept her goodwill—but at the expense of efficiency during a crucial time. What he was really saying to his

Associate Professor of Management, Hofstra University

110

fellow manager was: "How can I say 'No' to my subordinates when necessary and *still* keep their goodwill?"

Resentment guaranteed

It isn't easy. No matter how you say it, *no is no,* and the employee may still be resentful over the refusal. But some managers virtually guarantee such resentment by the way they deliver their refusals. Their very anticipation of an employee's anger and their own conflict over saying "No" may bring on a curt rejection scarcely calculated to soothe the frustrated subordinate.

Other managers use a delay technique. They'll say "Maybe," or "I'll look into it and let you know." If they are honestly undecided and want time to make up their mind, this is a legitimate approach. But too often it is simply a way of weaseling, of buying time in the hope that somehow the unpleasant duty of saying "No" can be avoided indefinitely.

Taking out the sting

There are ways to say "No" that make your refusal perfectly clear, yet remove a lot of the sting. Let's take the case of the requested time off, for example. The manager, under pressure to get out a rush order, dismissed his clerk's request in a peremptory manner that brought her to tears. Understandably, he felt that her request was a masterpiece of mistiming, and he reacted accordingly. If he had reflected for a moment before barking out a refusal, he would have recognized that in the mind of an employee a personal need may loom larger than a department need. Whether or not he agreed with his clerk's request, he should have tried to understand the point of view that caused it. If he had, he might have said something like this:

"I know it's difficult when there's no one home to take an important delivery, and I'd like to give you the time off today if I could. The trouble is, we do have to get this rush order out today—if we don't, we're going to fall seriously behind schedule, which would be especially bad with the Christmas holidays coming up. You're a key person—we'll never get the job done without you, so I just can't let you go. But I have a suggestion. Why don't you call the store and postpone the delivery till Friday? By that time the big push will be over, and we can spare you for a few hours."

Of course, the unhappy clerk still might have burst into tears—but at least her boss would have done what he could do to ease the blow of the refusal. First, he took her request seriously instead of giving it a curt brush-off. Second, he showed her that he understood how important the furniture delivery was to her. Third, he patiently explained just why it was not possible to grant her request. Fourth, he boosted her morale by letting her know he thought she was a key employee. And fifth, he offered an alternative solution to her with the delivery of her furniture.

Let's look at another situation—this one involving a request for a pay increase. A research technician walks into his boss's office one morning.

"As of today, I've been here six months. So far as I know, I've been doing a good job and I'd like to put in for a raise."

"Sorry, it can't be done. You're not eligible for a raise until you've been here nine months. I'll be glad to consider it then."

The manager probably doesn't mean to sound this harsh—he may be under pressure, in a bad mood, or embarrassed about having to turn down the request. But all the employee understands is that his request has been given a quick putdown. He's likely to retaliate for this rebuff by putting in less effort, turning other employees against the manager, or even looking for another job. In any case, the manager has probably lost a potentially valuable employee.

Constructive discussion

He could have handled the request differently.

"You're right, you have been doing a good job. I particularly liked the work you did on that Z-2 model last month—it was first-rate. But there are two reasons that I can't put in a recommendation for a raise right now. The first is company policy—you may have forgotten that employees aren't eligible for raises until they've been here nine months. Second, although I'm satisfied with your overall performance, there are several areas in which I would like to see some definite improvement before I recommend a raise for you. I had been intending to discuss them with you soon, but since you've brought up the question of a raise, now would be a good time. I'm sure that if you and I sit down now and work out some improvement goals for you to shoot at, I'll be able to recommend a merit increase for you in three months."

Here, the manager has turned what could have been a completely negative confrontation into a constructive discussion. The technician's request has been rejected, but he won't leave his boss's office empty-handed—he's been told he's doing a good job and he has a clearly defined set of improvement goals that will help him get his raise.

Basics of a tactful "No"

Every time you must say "No" to a subordinate's request, you will have to adapt your approach to the specific situation. But there are certain basic steps you can generally follow in order to reduce resentment and prevent low morale. Here's a rundown:

1. Listen patiently until your subordinate has finished making his request—even if you know before he's halfway through that you'll have to refuse it.

2. Try to find out more about the request and what's behind it. You may discover that it's based on a misunderstanding that needs clearing up.

3. When you make your reply, start out by showing your subordinate that you take his request seriously and realize that it's important to him.

4. Give a thorough explanation of the reasons that you must turn down the request—they may be obvious to you, but your subordinate may be completely unaware of them. Point out the specific effects that granting the request would have on production, morale, safety, or other areas.

5. Explore alternative solutions to the problem that inspired the request.

6. Tell your subordinate under what circumstances you could grant his request in the future and what he can do to bring those circumstances about.

7. Treat you subordinate normally after you've rejected his request. If you butter him up or act apologetic, he'll think you're feeling guilty about doing a rotten thing to him.

8. Be candid—it's better for morale in the long run. Your subordinate will resent transparent attempts to sidestep or sugarcoat the unpleasantness.

(Reprinted from SUPERVISORY MANAGEMENT, April 1970)

Allen Weiss

Do Your Instructions Get Lost in Translation?

HERB GREEN slammed the door to his office. Somebody's head is going to roll, he thought. Too many things had happened that day to credit coincidence.

First a customer called about a shipment that should have been made two days earlier. It was late despite the fact that Herb had gone out of his way to instruct the billing clerks himself.

Then Data Processing sent up a sales report that was exactly what Herb did not want. It was surely no accident, thought Herb, that the report excluded the very information that he had asked for.

Herb's secretary was away (she had always handled these matters for him), and her replacement was creating additional problems. Herb had clearly asked her to get a December report from the files, but she had come back with a November report.

After that, the Accounting Department called for a clarification of instructions that Herb had given them earlier. It seemed that four accountants had come up with two conflicting interpretations of what Herb had written.

The last straw

Now a minor incident was making Herb look foolish around the company. One of his memos had been sent by airmail to a department downstairs; the people there thought it was hilarious, of course, and they were spreading the story.

Reflecting on these events, Herb didn't really believe that he could be blamed for any of them. But then again, four accountants were waiting for clarification: That did raise a doubt. What had he told them?

The memo to the accountants read, in part: "In comparing earnings for the various divisions, take out bonuses and nonrecurring expenses." Two accountants thought that this meant to show divisional earnings with reductions for bonuses and nonrecurring expenses. The other two disagreed; in their view, the memo was a request to not count these charges, which were normally included in expenses, and thereby show higher earnings.

Two different meanings

How about the customer order?

Surely he had been explicit there. "See that this order goes out today," were his exact words to the billing section. But the billing people evidently thought that Herb meant "out of your department" because they said that they felt they had made good when they processed the order immediately and sent it to the shipping department—where it was routinely awaiting its turn.

Alerted to the possibility that something was wrong with the instructions he had been giving, Herb called Data Processing to ask them to repeat what he had told them about the sales run. They quoted him as having said, "Sort out the territories on a list I am sending you, and get me a sales run." So they selected out the territories on Herb's list and proceeded to run a report on the rest of the company's sales. Herb had neglected to tell them which sales to run.

What about the new secretary who brought Herb a November report instead of the December one? The transmittal letter she brought him was dated December, but the accompanying report covered November's activities. For the December information he wanted, Herb needed the next report—the one issued in January. How was a new secretary to know that?

Concerning the memo airmailed downstairs, Herb believed he was in the clear. True, he had said, "Send these copies by airmail to all sales offices and personnel departments." But he had expected the mailboy to use his head on as simple a matter as handling local mail. He was right to expect this.

How to say what you mean

Nevertheless, Herb learned two things from the day's experiences. First, he realized that he needed to make his directions more explicit and to take into account the listener's frame of reference. An uninstructed secretary may go by the date on a letter of transmittal rather than by the period covered in the accompanying report. A billing clerk may think in terms of billing, not shipping. When a computer operator sees instructions to pull something out of a file, he may interpret the word "out" literally and simply remove that information.

Second, Herb could see more clearly how faulty communications prolong the breaking-in period for a new employee and make it more difficult. When precise communication is habitual, training is that much easier.

Rapport is vital

One additional point should be mentioned. The mishandling of the mail was no accident, but a vengeful act on the part of the mailboy. He had resented the abrupt way Herb gave the instructions and, to get even, he applied them even to the local memo, which he knew should be delivered by hand.

Without exploring the rights and wrongs of the case, we can see that a supervisor must always remember amenities when he gives an order, for subordinates are highly sensitive to the spirit in which an order is given. A moderately sharp tone or an abrupt manner—stemming, perhaps, simply from preoccupation—may seem harsh and offensive. Carelessness that provokes an employee's resentment can cripple all future communication with him: When a subordinate is resentful, even the most precise orders may be intentionally misconstrued.

(Reprinted from SUPERVISORY MANAGEMENT, May 1970)

William Lefsky

Seven Steps to Giving Clear Instructions

DID YOU EVER tell someone what you wanted done, leave, and then return an hour later to find him still puzzling over how to begin? Or find that he had to do the job again because he did it wrong the first time?

Such problems can happen to any employee; but they happen most commonly to the new one. Typically, the new employee listens intently to your instructions, nodding to show that he understands. Meanwhile, he has doubts that he will not voice. He may not be sure what is confusing him or how to word a question. And since he is new and doesn't want to seem stupid, he'll gamble that he can figure out what you want done. At other times, he may believe that he does understand—only to discover the gaps in his knowledge when he actually tries to do the job.

These long delays and false starts do more than cause frustration. They may also consume valuable operating time, materials, and supplies and prevent other employees from performing at their best. Proper training can alleviate such problems by getting the new employee into his job faster and with less confusion. Here's how you can make your training more effective:

Methods Analyst, Abraham & Straus Division, Federated Department Stores, Inc.

1. *Find out what the employee already knows.* You may assume that an operation that is simple for you is simple for everyone, forgetting the difficulties you encountered in learning the job. You may further assume that anyone in your line of work has had the same experiences, which is not necessarily so. As a result, you may start with Step Six in the instructions, when the new employee is not yet ready for Step Three.

To compound the problems, you may begin your explanations thinking that you and the trainee share a common vocabulary. The trainee, however, might use a different word for the same operation, or the same word for a different one. And he might have learned to perform the same job in a different manner. Because assumptions like these make your training less effective, it is important to be aware of possible differences in viewpoint and the problems they can cause. Misunderstandings are bound to arise, but you can reduce their frequency by pinning down what the employee already knows and start teaching from there.

2. *Give a reason-why explanation.* Whenever practical, tell the employee why his particular job is important. You may feel too rushed to give these details and, at times, a bare explanation may be sufficient for getting the employee to do the job. However, few supervisors are willing to forgo the benefits that a fuller explanation provides. What are these benefits?

- *Retention.* The trainee is more likely to remember your instructions when he can relate them to the purpose of his task.
- *Morale.* Even if the trainee doesn't care why he is doing the job, he will be pleased that you bothered to explain it to him.
- *Cooperation.* If he knows the end use of his work, he will feel more like a member of the team.
- *Performance.* Knowing the purpose of his work will enable him to think of possible improvements and, since no instructions can cover all contingencies, the new employee is more likely to take the right actions if unforeseen circumstances occur.

3. *Show an example or illustration.* When misunderstanding is possible and the cost of confusion is potentially high—whether in time, money, or employee self-esteem—it pays to show the new employee an example of what he is to do. A case in point is the supervisor who wanted a report typed to the same format as an earlier one. Not wanting to take the time to locate the earlier report in the files, he described in words how he wanted the new typist to arrange the report.

After spending 30 minutes figuring out what he wanted, she used her common sense and arranged the report in what she felt was a logical format. Then she presented the completed report to her supervisor.

The "logical" layout was not what he wanted. He then searched the files, pulled the earlier report, and told her to retype the manuscript to look like the earlier report. If he had done this in the first place, of course, they wouldn't have wasted so much time. And the typist wouldn't have become angry, as she did in this instance, at a boss who penalized her for his own mistakes.

4. *Make it clear that you welcome questions.* "Why didn't you listen when I answered that question yesterday?" is a sure-fire way to block questions—and learning. You can get similar results with comments like "It's plain common sense. . . ." or "Anyone knows that this is the way. . . ."

The trainee who feels that he can ask a question without being humiliated will let you know what he must yet learn. He will be more willing to help you help him avoid wasted time and costly mistakes.

5. *Watch at the start and recheck early in the job.* Generally you will want to watch a new employee as he begins a task and then check soon after he is into the work. As he progresses, you may let him begin the job by himself and do your checking a little after he starts. When you have full confidence in him, you will just spot-check. Naturally, if the job is an important one and the consequences of error are great, you should check on the employee earlier than you would if the consequences were minor.

In conducting these spot checks, you will probably find it necessary to correct the employee. When you must correct him, do so without being unnecessarily harsh. Remember—you are clearing up a misunderstanding and broadening the employee's training, not reprimanding him for errors that he's too new to catch himself. If he's doing the job right, let him know that, too.

6. *Give the employee a sense of success.* This is one of a trainer's most important functions because it is the self-confidence born of success that keeps the learner alert and eager to take on greater challenges. Of course, there are times when even your best employee will botch a job. Do not make a big issue of occasional failures. Instead, try to guide the employee through a series of successful experiences aimed at building his sense of accomplishment. You can do this by starting the trainee on easy jobs and giving him progressively more difficult ones over a period of time.

7. *Have him practice his new skills.* Some jobs are just barely learned, done once or twice, then laid aside for a month or more. Then, when the employee is asked to do the job again, he finds—to his dismay—that he's forgotten how.

These experiences need not occur if you give the trainee the opportunity to learn a job thoroughly. Drill him in the job until it becomes second nature to him. You might also have him set up step-by-step instructions as a future reminder.

This training sequence is effective with experienced employees also. Whether you have to teach a new skill or procedure or simply remind people of the old ones, you'll find it helpful to follow these six steps to better training.

(Reprinted from SUPERVISORY MANAGEMENT, June 1971)

Brooks Mitchell

Let Your Subordinates Be in the Know

IN SOME CASES, withholding information from employees is justified. However, withholding too much information can be detrimental to departmental effectiveness, especially if your organization is trying to encourage participative management. Simply stated, participative management seeks to narrow the gulf between supervisors and subordinates by having employees at all levels of the organization help formulate decisions that affect their jobs.

The strength of the system is that it gives people a bigger stake in their work, a greater responsibility for planning and controlling their activities. Consequently, participative management can stimulate morale and productivity *if* employees have access to information they need to do the planning and controlling.

In a participative-management system, one of the supervisor's primary responsibilities is to see that employees get this information. Withhold the necessary information, and the benefits of participation will dissolve. Dr. Don Wass, Manager of Components Training and Development at Texas Instruments Incorporated, illustrates the importance of fluid communication in the following incident:

"It was the end of the billing period in a certain electronics firm.

Assistant Personnel Director, Core Laboratories

The second-shift foreman reported to work in the shipping department. He was told by the day-shift foreman that everything he could ship before midnight could be sold. The second-shift foreman acknowledged the information and, in turn, encouraged his people to go the extra mile in shipping all the units they could inspect. By midnight he had shipped 50 percent more units than was judged normal. He felt very pleased that his people had responded so well to his request.

"Naturally, he was shocked when he reported to work the next day and was informed by his boss that he had really 'blown it' the previous night. The boss was very upset because the second-shift foreman had shipped primarily units with a $.20 gross-profit margin, while the $3.00 gross-profit margin units had remained untouched. When questioned as to why he had allowed this to happen, his reply was 'Nobody told me what the profit was on the devices.' "

His boss felt that gross-profit margin was not the kind of information you give to everyone because it could damage the firm's competitive position. Paradoxically, however, by keeping the information locked in his desk, he had accomplished precisely what he had hoped to prevent.

Information: a status symbol?

According to Mason Haire, Alfred P. Sloan Professor of Management at MIT, a degree of information hoarding goes on at all levels of management. One reason is that having information or access to it affords one a certain prestige. A supervisor is expected to know more than his subordinates know. And some supervisors maintain their information leverage by telling subordinates "only what they need to know."

In some instances, the supervisor's boss may also hoard information. This can lead to a situation where, to cover up his lack of knowledge, a supervisor may try to act *as if* he knows certain withheld information. More than once such ploys have backfired when the supposedly confidential information has been made public. A typical countermove by the supervisor is to act as if he knows some *other* important information.

What are the results?

There is nothing wrong with a supervisor's wanting to satisfy his ego. Some behavioral scientists say ego satisfaction may be a primary reason for striving to get ahead in an organization. However, a supervisor who gratifies his own information needs at the expense of his subordinates' information needs may well be striking the death blow at participative management, a blow that could result in:

• *Mistrust.* If you continually withhold information from subordinates, they will feel that you don't trust them and perhaps that they should not trust you, either. Adding to the damage that suspicion causes is the damage caused by what psychologists call the *self-fulfilling prophecy.* People behave as you expect them to. If, for example, you believe that your subordinates can't be trusted with information, your behavior will project your conviction and will, in a sense, encourage subordinates to act in untrustworthy ways.

The way to dispel the fear and mistrust, of course, is to change your assumptions. Naturally you can't reveal all the information at your disposal. But by taking steps toward being more open with subordinates and giving them a chance to prove that they can handle the information in a mature and responsible way, you can build a climate that encourages productive and cooperative behavior.

• *Rumors.* Lacking information they want or need, people usually interpret facts and events in a way that makes sense to them. A person who sees his environment as hostile and threatening, for example, will fill in information gaps with threatening and hostile assumptions. This is how rumors are created. If you don't tell people the facts, they decide the ''facts'' for themselves.

Supervisors try in many ways to counteract false rumors. One technique is to get at the source—which is usually the grapevine. It is not surprising that most supervisors view the grapevine with suspicion, blaming it for distortions and misinformation. To stifle rumors, they may simply say less in the expectation that the less information they pass on, the less active the grapevine will be.

In reality, however, the reverse happens. The more information you withhold, the more you arouse subordinates' suspicions and the more they rely on the grapevine to find out what's happening.

• *Rigid hierarchy.* We all need certain information to do our jobs adequately. In an informal department, subordinates feel free to seek information where it is most likely to be found, even if it means going outside their own department. If, for example, a laboratory technician needs information from the R&D manager, he can go directly to that man to find out what he needs to know.

When such informal communication networks are blocked—if, for example, the R&D manager will talk only to the technician's supervisor—one of two things may happen: The technician may, at the expense of his own performance, stop trying to get the information. Or he may ask his supervisor to spend valuable time getting it for him. In the latter case, the R&D manager's reply must pass through a chain of command before it reaches the technician. The longer the chain, the greater the possibility that information will be distorted or misunderstood. Too rigid a hierarchy inhibits, rather than promotes, organizational effectiveness.

Too meager a flow of information can have similar results. Especially in a department that is trying to encourage participation, subordinates need reliable and timely information to be able to work most effectively. A supervisor in the process of studying his department's information needs would do well to ask: Do I really need to keep that information to myself? His answer could be revealing and helpful.

(Reprinted from SUPERVISORY MANAGEMENT, April 1971)

Jesse S. Nirenberg

Solving the Problems of Persuasion
1. How to Create a Receptive Attitude

ARRIVING AT A GOOD IDEA, especially after considerable thought, analysis, and weighing of alternatives, is always a gratifying experience. However, the idea will never be translated into action if you can't convince others of its validity and advantages. Techniques of communication must be called into play to gain their acceptance and backing of the idea—to guide their thinking through the barriers of resistance to change, inner distractions, preconceptions, and ego needs. In presenting your case you must first gain full attention; then feed in ideas for maximum learning by the other person; maintain thought continuity; see that there is clear understanding of your own and the other's positions; give and gain insight into implications; and together weigh one side against the other.

Consulting psychologist to industry

Motivating to listen

Almost anyone will listen to a clear statement of what he stands to gain. If, instead, the conversation begins with a question, the listener is pushed into a conversation without knowing whether he has any interest in it.

It is a mistake to treat anyone merely as a source of information to be maneuvered into the desired response; rather, he should be considered an equal partner in the thinking and in the conclusion it leads to, because his self-esteem is involved. A question should be prefaced by the reason for asking it; the objectives of a discussion should be made clear before it starts.

Suppose a manager starts a conversation with a subordinate by asking him how far along he is on Project A. Because the subordinate does not know what the manager is getting at, he is likely to become wary, defensive, guarded.

Suppose, on the other hand, the manager opens up his thinking to the subordinate, saying: "We've just been given a high-priority project to complete in three months. At the same time, I'd like to keep on schedule with Project A. If necessary, I'll get you some help. How far along are you with Project A?" Now that the subordinate knows the purpose, he will probably open up and provide answers to the manager's questions. Moreover, because people have a problem-solving propensity, he will volunteer information that the manager might not have thought to ask about, in an attempt to help solve the problem.

Maintaining thought continuity

If you want to persuade, remember how people learn. Each idea in a series tends to make the learner forget previous ones, so it is better to give him one idea at a time.

Feedback is essential in maintaining thought continuity. Encouraging discussion of the idea involves two learning processes: For one thing, it requires repetition, and people learn in proportion to the amount of repetition. Second, discussion requires effort, and people retain in proportion to the amount of effort they invest in learning.

Studies show that people listen selectively, hearing what they want to hear, blocking what they don't, and they also reshape what they hear to make it conform to preconceptions. Feedback helps determine what the listener has absorbed and cues the next move.

For example, one man says, "I can see how this new procedure will save us money, but I don't think it's going to work. Our people have been doing it the old way and they won't change. They're not going to want to learn a new set of instructions and then worry about making mistakes."

The other answers, "We're going to set up a training program to show them just how to do it so they won't make mistakes."

Here, an impression of continuity is given because there is a connection between introducing a new procedure and conducting a training program for its operation. However, the first person is talking not about mastering the new procedure, but about the employees' willingness to do so. He is talking about motivation, not about training, and therefore the second person should have responded in the same vein: "I think we can sell them on this new procedure by showing them how much easier their jobs will be and how they will wind up making fewer mistakes."

Implanting ideas

If a person is to accept information presented to him by another, he must be receptive to ideas. In an inquiring state of mind, he is open to ideas, but if he is in an objecting or resisting state, he will tune out or selectively distort incoming information.

The demands of his self-esteem often move a person to minimize or reject outright arguments that run counter to his own position. If the argument outweighs his own, he will logically have to change his position; but if he has just committed himself to this position, reversing it immediately might make him feel unstable in his thinking, doubtful of his judgment. Moreover, taking a new position can in itself be threatening because of the unknown elements. As a result, he is inclined to shut out the other's arguments rather than contend with lowered self-esteem and the threat of something untried.

It follows that, when he encounters an objection, instead of trying to achieve an immediate about-face, the man who is seeking agreement should draw out the other, expressing understanding of his position, recognizing whatever merits it has, conceding that such an idea under some circumstances might be reasonable, and then asking for consideration of the alternative ideas. When the other man asks a question or otherwise indicates interest or approval, he is open to outside ideas;

again, they should be given one at a time, with a response drawn after each idea is presented.

No ego damage

The other person may be taking his first good look at his position when he is asked to explain why he feels that something won't work or is too expensive. It may be that he simply didn't want to change or didn't want to spend money. However, telling him at this point why the other course will work or why it isn't too expensive is usually jumping the gun. It is more effective first to invite him to explain his viewpoint and thus force him to test the soundness of his logic's underpinnings. In trying to grasp the substance of his own reasoning to pass it along, he finds his position untenable. Now he needs a new position, and to fill the void you can lead him to yours.

Always give the reasoning behind your position. Don't just describe what your idea does that the other does not; tell how or why your idea does it.

(Reprinted from SUPERVISORY MANAGEMENT, June 1968)

2. How to Find Out What People Are Really Saying

AN INITIAL STATEMENT is often only a vague approximation of what a person means, because people have a tendency to think aloud, to grope toward their meaning; yet their hearers often respond as if it were precisely what the other person means. To illustrate, someone may object that a suggested procedure is too complicated. The inclination would be to explain immediately that the procedure is really not complicated, that it requires a series of quite simple steps.

However, drawing out the balky critic may very well reveal that it isn't the complexity per se that bothers him; he is really concerned about resistance from people under him who would not want to give up a familiar, well-learned procedure and go to the trouble of learning a new one that has not proved its worth.

Similarly, when a conversation opens with a generalization, such as, "Too many people get involved in every decision made around here," the person who disagrees will probably come back with another generalization, such as, "Several heads are better than one for many decisions, so we might as well draw on all the talent available.'' Actually, the person who made the first comment may have had in mind one particular incident that caused trouble rather than the group decision-making process in general.

To avoid the inevitable misunderstandings that arise in an exchange of generalized statements, ask the other person to explain his generalization further and give an example. As for yourself, avoid talking in generalizations when you have a specific in mind. Don't say, ''We need a change in design,'' when you only want to make something round rather than square. True, this is a design change, but the phrase ''change in design'' is too sweeping, and may instantly produce a negative reaction. The person you are talking to may be thinking about some entirely different aspect than a change from squareness to roundness, and he also may have built up a conditioned reaction to the word change. Words designating broad categories, like *change, organization, decision, future, advancement,* have emotional associations that make people wary when they crop up.

Interpreting

Insight into what another person really means can often be gained by interpreting to him the implication of what he is saying. This dialogue illustrates the interpreting process:

''I want you to do everything possible to get this job out on time.''

''Does this mean that I can hire more people?''

''Well, no. We would have the problem of letting people go after the job is done, which would make for bad public relations, or we'd have the problem of finding other jobs for them.''

''Then can I work my people overtime to any extent that seems necessary?''

''Well, we've got to watch our budget. We could probably take a certain amount of overtime, but maybe you'd better check with me on just how much overtime you want.''

Here, interpreting back and forth helped both men realize that the words ''everything possible'' in the original statement weren't really meant and that limits had to be defined.

This questioning form of interpretation is another way of drawing out, and drawing out in any form not only clarifies the other person's meaning, but also gives him greater insight into his own wants.

Weighing

In all decision making there is a weighing of advantages against disadvantages, and this weighing requires the assignment of values to the various pro and con elements.

Values are often arbitrarily made up to favor a desired conclusion. Suppose there is a question of spending money for a project with a long-range and even somewhat uncertain return. Realistically, a person should first calculate as accurately as he can the ratio of return to investment, the time required to achieve the return, and the probability of success, using estimates if no definite figures are available. However, he may have a generalized anxiety about spending money, and the prospect of feeling anxiety over a long period of time leads him to veto the project. He then rationalizes his decision by unconsciously assigning inflated values to the disadvantages and wishfully diminished values to the advantages.

The use of adjectives and adverbs adds to this wishful distortion. Descriptive terms—like *efficient, expensive, durable, economical,* and *timesaving*—cover a whole range of values and therefore have different meanings to different people. Adjectives and adverbs should be used very sparingly in business conversation. Whenever you hear an adjective or adverb, ask the person using it to tell you what quantity he means, to be specific, or to give an example. Consider this dialogue:

"I think we ought to try this approach because it's more efficient."

"Maybe so, but it's too expensive."

"But we'll save in the long run."

"But it will cause a lot of trouble."

"Not if we introduce it properly."

"There are too many places it can go wrong."

This interchange could go on endlessly, but boils down to yes it is—no it isn't—yes it is—no it isn't, simply because no weighing is possible without quantifying or specifying the criterion of efficiency, how much money is involved, how long the "long run" is, how much trouble is involved, how the approach would be introduced, and what and how many snags there are. It is difficult for anyone to dismiss a new approach when he is told that the advantages weighed against the disadvantages would result in a net saving of $10,000 a year and that he therefore would be paying this amount for following the old way.

The need to be rational

People want very much to be rational. If they didn't, they wouldn't go to such lengths to justify a position that they secretly, and uneasily, know is shaky. Caught between their wishes and fears on the one hand and the need to sound reasonable on the other, they often compromise by assigning exaggerated values to make the desired answer come out.

Once you work with another person to quantify as much as possible, however, he gains insight into the situation as it really is. His need to be rational has something concrete to work with and the obstacles he sees tend to lose their emotional load when he describes them in specific terms. Now he can make a more realistic decision.

Any persuasive conversation, whether in selling, negotiating, training, problem solving, or decision making, requires the use of these conversational techniques. Skill in using them requires self-discipline and self-awareness to counteract the old, ingrained habit of talking without communicating, but the reward is straight thinking and a meeting of minds.

(Reprinted from SUPERVISORY MANAGEMENT, July 1968)

Jack Danner

Don't Let the Grapevine Trip You Up

As OLIVER MANZINI drove home, he was deep in thought about the news he had heard that day and what he was going to do about it. Because the government space program was being phased out, Manzini's company had lost a major contract—one that had called for the production of integrated circuits for computers.

But things were not as bad as they had seemed at first, because the marketing department had anticipated the loss more than a year before. To head off the bad effects of a drop in sales, the sales manager had contracted with two major computer manufacturers to provide the two with the same integrated circuits, only slightly modified, that the company had been supplying to the government. The modification required a change in two machines that were used in producing the circuits, so the machines would have to be shut down for two weeks while Maintenance made the necessary adjustments. During the shutdown, 30 workers—all of them under Manzini's supervision—would have to be temporarily laid off.

As he approached his house, Manzini was pondering the best approach for telling his subordinates about the change so that they would understand and accept the layoff as well as possible. He knew that if

Personnel Supervisor, Formex Company, Division of Huyck Corporation

the employees were not properly informed, rumors would circulate and the situation could turn into a real problem.

As Manzini entered the house, his wife hurried to greet him. "Oh, Honey," she said. "I just heard. It's so terrible! Will it affect you?" Naturally, he did a double take. He ran through several events of that day to try to figure out what his wife was talking about, but finally had to ask her to explain.

"I'm talking about the big layoff," she said. "Jane heard about it at the beauty parlor and called me right away. She was so worried that they would let you go. It's all over town now that your company has lost all of its government contracts and will have to close down most of its operations at that plant. The way you looked when you came up the walk, I just knew you had been laid off."

Word is passed

The example above illustrates that the grapevine is able to flow so quickly inside and outside of a company that it reaches people before formal (company) communications can. The rumor grapevine—the communication arm of the informal organization—is a by-product of human communication that often begins in an effort to provide an emotional safety valve for frustrations or worries. In fact, it has been said that the grapevine is first as the medium of communication, followed by the supervisor and the memo. Generally, rumors are not developed as deliberate lies, but are usually begun to satisfy the need for information. Most people find rumors credible because they contain truths or half-truths. Naturally, in some instances, rumors may be completely false, but since they usually develop either from actual facts that have leaked or from circumstantial evidence, rumors usually contain an element of truth.

Often, as in the example above concerning job security, employees who fear the loss of their jobs band together for the recognition and support that they should be getting from management. While you must accept the inevitability of the grapevine's existence, you should be up to date on the power it wields and the way it operates in your unit so that you'll be able to work with it. You occupy a strategic position in communication channels because you can transmit, filter, or block two-way communication between higher management and your subordinates. It behooves you to get the grapevine on your side and establish communication procedures to make the most of your position.

What ignites a rumor?

If a rumor is to have a path along which to run, the original story must be important to its communicators. Another part of this theory is that when important news is not communicated properly, when information is blocked, when versions conflict, or when information is withheld, people look for a reasonable explanation—and they look for it in rumors. To further delineate the grapevine, studies show that rumors travel best when they are confirming the worst fears or when they are painting the rosiest of pictures.

Formal communication meets the needs of the formal organization, whereas informal communication provides an opportunity to participate in social activities that are not "programmed." Often, the vast network of procedures and committees that brings workers together gives the grapevine as many arms as an octopus has. And while informal channels of communication are not always oriented to the goals of the formal organization, they do satisfy the personal objectives of the people who are spreading the rumors.

Serial transmission and gobbledegook

As the word is passed, consider the serial transmission of a story. Often, we chop off important details that would put a different light on the story. Other times, details seem to spoil the punch that a story might have, so we omit them. Let's go back to the example when Jane was interpreting to Manzini's wife the message that she heard at the beauty shop. Jane may have been trying to simplify the message, or she may have been trying to take the bite out of the message.

Sometimes we take the most conspicuous features of the story and strengthen them to make a better story. Often, we communicate only part of the story when we wish to avoid making that story too long or complex. Since passing along detailed information is difficult and untidy for us, we generally tend to omit some facts—frequently because we may assume that the listener already knows them anyway. Yet he may not know those facts that are essential to understanding the *whole* story.

As potential communicators of the messages we hear, we make every effort to rework those that aren't clear to us until we feel that we can convey information that is logical. But in making a message intelligible to ourselves, we might add a nuance that was missing and, in doing so, change at least the tone of the story.

William V. Haney conducted several experiments in serial communication. In his article, "Serial Communication of Informal Organizations," Haney describes the type of experiment we have all heard of and might have known as "telephone." In form, it works much the way the chain letter does. That is, it is spread widely once it is started, it is changed with each transmission, and it eventually dies because of lack of interest. Here's how serial communication goes. A message is read to the first person, who in turn passes his interpretation to the next person, who passes it to the third person, and so on until it has been passed to the last person in the series, who then relates the final version for comparison with the original message.

The original story Haney used in one experiment is as follows: "Every year at State University, the eagles in front of the Psi Gamma fraternity house were mysteriously sprayed during the night. Whenever this happened, it cost the Psi Gams from $75 to $100 to have the eagles cleaned. The Psi Gams complained to officials and were promised by the president of the university that if any students were caught painting the eagles, they would be expelled from school."

Here are some examples of the more distorted versions of the story; they illustrate how bizarre rumors can become, bearing little resemblance to the original story. "At a state university there was an argument between two teams—the Eagles and the Fire Gems—in which their clothing was torn." Another account was: "The eagles in front of the university had parasites and were sprayed with insecticide." Another version: "At State U., a flock of birds were desecrating buildings. To remedy the situation, administrators expelled the students who fed the birds." And the last version: "The White House was in such a mess that the members wanted to renovate it, but they found that the cost would be from $75 to $100 to paint the eagle, so they decided against it."

Everyone is aware of the grapevine's existence. Among its characteristics are that it is often faster than formal communications; it's influential; it's often incorrect; it can be useful where formal communication is inappropriate; and it can exert pressure on members of the informal group. Considering that it is so widely discussed, the grapevine is, ironically enough, one of the most neglected mediums of communication. As a carrier of news and gossip, the grapevine often indirectly affects the affairs of the company from top management down. Some supervisors feel that no good can come of the grapevine—that it only spreads rumors, destroys morale and reputations, and upstages the formal channels of communication. Others feel that when the grapevine is properly controlled, it can act as a safety valve for frustrations and carry news quickly. Still others view the grapevine with mixed feelings.

There is merit in each point of view. Whether the grapevine is good or bad depends on what kind you have. At times the grapevine can pass along rumors, destroy reputations, and wreck morale. But the grapevine can also be a useful supplement to the formal channels of communication. And one thing is certain. It is each manager's job to bring the grapevine into closer harmony with the total needs of the organization and work group.

Most studies of the grapevine show that a department will wind up with the kind of grapevine it deserves. These grapevines thrive on three kinds of rumors: anxiety rumors, wish-fulfillment rumors, and wedge-driving rumors. Anxiety rumors make dire and specific predictions that reflect general uneasiness among employees; wish-fulfillment rumors are merely those that spring from wishful thinking; and wedge-driving rumors are the deliberate or unconscious expressions of disunity in or between employees or departments. The vulnerability of any group to rumors is in direct proportion to the strength of that group's leadership.

Where communication failed

The Miles Automatic Weaving Company was not successful in communicating with its employees. Any information the company wanted passed along to employees would usually be posted on the bulletin board. Front-line supervisors were often ill-informed, and when they did have access to information, they were afraid to pass it on for fear that they would have to answer questions or that *they* might start rumors. Let's see how the grapevine at Miles Automatic Weaving Company tried to satisfy the needs of the employees for information, but failed.

The company was planning to automate its payroll department. In no time, the rumor spread that the company was getting a computer and that the company would not need any clerical help once the computer was functioning. When they received this tidbit, most of the clerical employees left the company and sought jobs in other companies for what they considered to be better job security.

In the same company later that year, rumors based on wishful thinking sprang up when an employee asked his supervisor if the company would be giving bonuses at the end of the year. The supervisor knew that there had been no bonuses in the past, and that there was no reason to think there would be any that year. But, thinking that the employee might know something he didn't, he noncommittally said, "I'm not saying yes and I'm not saying no." The supervisor was amazed to find out later that he was quoted as the *source* of the rumor that the company would be giving a big bonus that year. Morale in the company dropped when employees found that this was not true.

Control

Rumors and the grapevine can be controlled—but not completely controlled. That is, rumors can be kept to a minimum or can be stopped before they get out of hand. You can control rumors most effectively if you learn to analyze the anxieties behind them, and if you can use the grapevine in conjunction with formal channels of communication.

Most rumors can be traced back to a breakdown in formal and semiformal communication channels. A breakdown might begin when a memorandum is not clear to all employees, or when not everyone gets the same message from letters sent to them at home. Once a message is misunderstood, don't try to disprove the rumor; just present facts to bring out the true story. Keep in mind that while subordinates set them afoot, you have the authority to dispel those rumors—and often you can do so by clarifying policies. After all, you are expected to be able to answer questions and consistently interpret each policy. For example, when employees begin asking about raises around the time of the year when wage increases are usually announced, they expect reasonable answers. You may not be able to reveal the package policy to them, because it may not have been approved yet. But there are reasonable answers that you can and should give them, if you want to prevent the grapevine from stepping in and obliging.

If you have established a good working relationship with subordinates, you will know what the grapevine is spreading. And if the relationship is one of mutual trust, employees frequently keep you informed of rumors on the grapevine. When they do confront you, they will be looking for verification of facts, so it's important that you be prepared to provide them with facts and timely feedback.

Unfortunately, the realities of life are such that there are no ideal situations or clear-cut cases that follow a given pattern of solution. For example, suppose information is confidential. Even though you feel a need to communicate, you realize that you must remain silent. But before the grapevine takes over, get in touch with your boss to let him know what subordinates and others are saying. This will give top management an opportunity to sort out any details that *can* be given to employees. In the meantime, be prepared to answer certain questions that employees are bound to ask. Or, if you prefer, call in your key employees and give them the information; talk it over with them and get their reactions. Then you'll be assured that the right word will be passed along—and you'll get feedback that will cue you on other facts you need.

In any case, don't distort information by "softening" it if it is bad, or by playing it up too much if it is good. This means facing the situation as it really exists. But in talking with subordinates, don't openly discuss your opposition to a stand that management has taken. Doing so might make you the hero of the moment, but eventually you will be looked upon as an "outsider" of the management team by those same awestricken subordinates.

(Reprinted from SUPERVISORY MANAGEMENT, November 1972)

Jack Danner

"But I Assumed..."

A BIOLOGY PROFESSOR spent ten years training a flea to jump on command. When he had it trained, he began removing one leg at a time from the flea. Each time he removed a leg, he would command it to jump—which it did, slowly. Finally, when he commanded it to jump after the last leg was removed, it did nothing. The professor concluded that when all the legs were removed from the flea, it became deaf.

In this clearly apocryphal story, the professor's conclusion was wrong because his assumption was wrong. When a supervisor makes the wrong assumptions, it is a more serious matter. A supervisor's assumptions lead to actions that directly affect his subordinates, so he had better be sure that he makes the right ones. When a supervisor acts on the basis of wrong assumptions, he can adversely affect his subordinates' work or even lives and will decrease efficiency in his department, waste everybody's time, and end up making wrong decisions. Why do supervisors sometimes make the wrong assumptions? Assumptions may be wrong because the supervisor has failed to distinguish between fact and fiction, between facts and inconclusive observations, or between facts and inferences. The simple making of a statement does not mean that the statement is a fact. Many people accept statements as fact simply because they are statements.

Even direct observation can be inconclusive. For example, a supervisor leading a group at a seminar held up an object and asked all the participants to write down as many observations as they could within a limited amount of time. Everyone immediately wrote down that it was a pencil with black lead in it; it had a sharp point; it had a wood casing topped with a brass eraser holder; it was blue; and so on. The leader called time out, and the participants sat back, proud of the lists that they had compiled. Instead of calling on someone to go over the list, the teacher bent the pencil and flipped it around to show that it was a dummy pencil made of rubber.

Of course, it would be impossible to work or live from day to day without forming assumptions. You would not have enough time to move through your routine chores if you had to test every assumption that you have ever formed. When you see a chair, you assume that it will support you. When you see an open door, you assume that you will pass through it when you cross the threshold. When you read a job applicant's résumé, you assume that it is accurate.

Everybody plays the fool

There is obviously a fine line between what you can assume and what you should not assume. For example, the same group leader mentioned above asked participants to observe a slide for a short period of time. He asked the group to observe as much as possible about the slide. After he turned the slide off, he asked the group to write down what they had seen.

All the participants wrote down that they had seen three geometric shapes: a triangle, a circle, and a rectangle. They wrote that they had seen three well-known phrases, one in each geometric figure. In the triangle, they had seen *A Bird in the Hand*. In the circle, they had seen *Paris in the Springtime*. Finally, in the rectangle, they saw *Once in a Lifetime*.

The leader flashed the slide back on the screen. He asked everyone to look carefully at what was there. To the embarrassment of all, what was actually written in the shapes were the following statements: *A Bird in the the Hand, Paris in the the Springtime, Once in a a Lifetime*.

Having heard the phrases many times, everyone saw just enough of the phrases in the shapes to make an assumption about the completed phrases.

Because of a natural tendency to make assumptions, everyone has been the victim of such "teasers." But does this mean that you cannot rely on your assumptions? Not at all. What it means is that when your assumptions are based on incomplete information, there is a strong probability that you will be led astray. If your information is wrong, your assumptions will be wrong. If you base your information on facts that have been previously tested, then your assumptions will probably be right. But don't forget that I said *probably,* because in the case of the flea, the professor based his assumption on correct information and still drew the wrong conclusion.

Invisible fences make good neighbors, sometimes

Another way in which assumptions can interfere with communication shows up when you construct conscious or unconscious barriers that interfere with creativity and the open expression of ideas. After a while, you can become conditioned to assume that these barriers exist.

Every farmer who has put in an electric fence to restrain his cattle knows that by the second or third day, the electricity can be turned off. After the initial shock, the cattle assume that if they go too near the fence, they will be shocked. They have fixed the boundary of the pasture firmly in their minds. Are you that susceptible to habit?

Notice how in an office situation, where two people work side by side, there is an invisible line that divides their work stations. While there may be no physical barrier, watch what happens when they pack up to go home. You won't see them straightening up each other's papers.

In your day-to-day activities, you may place restrictions and boundaries on yourself that were not placed there by anyone else. When these boundaries are assumed, they restrict your effectiveness. But the construction of boundaries is not only a one-sided problem in communication. The people you communicate with may construct them, too. Let's say a foreman is passing a work bench and tells the worker that he had better get his area cleaned up. The worker might think that he means clean it up before going home. If the company president walked by and said the same thing, the worker would probably clean it up immediately.

The president might have had the same idea as the foreman, but because of the president's status in the company hierarchy, a different message was communicated. It's possible that the president was aware of his power or influence and used it to convey his message.

Are you a "know it all?"

One time, an assistant director was asked by his superior to write up a report and present his recommendations for updating the company's application forms. The assistant went to the library and found every book and article on the topic. He poured over page after page of instruction, theory, exhortation, labor laws, and personnel testing and hiring laws. When he felt that he knew more about the subject than anyone else, he prepared his report. Then he presented it to the personnel director.

Personnel director: "Well, I see you've done a good job of research. But I really disagree with you about your approach. For instance, on page 9. . . ."

The assistant butted in: "But in the GLU book on interviewing and personnel procedures, it says. . . ."

Personnel director: "Look, Harry, the problem is simply that you've hardly ever interviewed anyone. I've been in the business 25 years, and I still don't know everything there is to know. But certainly my experience tells me that some of your recommendations are unrealistic."

By thinking that he had all the right answers, the assistant left himself open to embarrassment. But because of the importance of the situation, he quickly reopened his mind. If he had presented his recommendations to his peers or to someone on a lower level, he probably would have felt that his word was conclusive. If he hadn't reopened his mind, he would never have heard any new ideas.

A "know-it-all" attitude tends to make a person become arrogant. It stops the process of observation when you assume away any constructive new ideas. Too many assumptions about anything can make you complacent in your search for knowledge and can create a serious impediment to effective communication.

Test your assumptions

You may not be able to test every assumption that you make in your daily life. But you can test some assumptions to ensure that you will communicate effectively. A simple way to test them—one that will help you stay on solid ground—is to ask effective questions.

Perry Mason fans may recall the time when he objected to a question on the grounds that the prosecutor was leading the witness. If you ask a question so that you end up leading a person to your way of thinking, you may win. And it may not be so bad if you were right to begin with. But what if your original assumptions were wrong? Your questions will not test these assumptions, but only reinforce them.

The only way to test an assumption is to find out how it was formed. Teachers have learned that questions can promote understanding of a subject. The more questions a student asks, the better chance he has of correcting his erroneous assumptions. The more information a person obtains, the more valid his conclusions will be. If you ask someone, "How do you know that?" you will find out more about his assumptions than if you disagree or accept them on the spot.

Let's say a new lathe operator handles the machine differently from the way his foreman had shown him how to run it. The foreman has two choices: He can ask the man why he runs the machine that way, or he can reprimand the worker for not following instructions. If the foreman does decide to ask the operator why he uses the machine in that manner, he may find out that he learned it in a training course at his previous plant. The worker may go on to explain why his method is superior to the other. In that case, the foreman will have benefited by not having given in to his original assumptions and by having asked "Why?"

When you ask questions to test your assumptions, make them gentle and go only deep enough to gather the necessary facts with which to draw a valid conclusion. Control your questions so that the answers won't stray. Keep them direct and to the point, and prepare the other person by letting him know why you are asking the questions. Questions are for clarification, not competition. Once you learn how to test your assumptions, you will be on the road to more effective communication.

(Reprinted from SUPERVISORY MANAGEMENT, January 1973)

Richard Stern

Better Human Relationships Through Better Communication

OUR CONCEPT of communication usually centers on a fairly set process: A message sender puts his message into oral or written words and sends it through the appropriate medium; the receiver reads or hears the message, interprets it according to his frame of reference, and gives a response. But this is just part of what happens when people communicate. In his book *On Human Communication,* Colin Cherry explains that communication is not simply the message you initiate or the response the listener gives. Rather, it is the *relationship* set up by the messages you send and the responses you receive.

Your relationship with subordinates is both a cause and an effect of your communicating effectiveness. It is a cause in that your disposition toward another person will color your interpretation of what he says. It is an effect because the messages you send and the manner in which you send them play a part in determining the response you receive. This explains one reason that communication is so important to a supervisor: Subordinates will be more responsive to him if he communicates effectively.

The role of human relationships in communication is illustrated in the following example: It was four o'clock and Supervisor John L.

President, Richard Stern Associates

asked Susan, his secretary, to type a three-page memo—a rush item that had just come up. Susan responded, "Why is it that everything around here is a rush? Nothing ever gets to me when I have the time—always at the last minute."

Sidetracking the issue

In this instance, Susan sidetracked communication in two ways: She brought up a topic unrelated to the memo. And in doing so, she momentarily blocked the supervisor from getting the memo typed.

This left John L. with two problems—the memo and tension between himself and Susan. Each required a separate solution. John's immediate problem was to have the memo finished, so he refocused the conversation by repeating the request: "Susan, will you please type this memo? I need it by 4:45." Susan looked disagreeable, but proceeded with the typing.

The remaining problem took longer to resolve. Talking with Susan gave the supervisor an opportunity to uncover the causes for the conflict between them. Their first talk took place the following morning—in private, of course. He began by commenting that he and Susan were not getting along as well as he would like, and that he wanted to iron out the difficulties—an approach that got Susan's confirmation that a problem existed. With the problem out in the open, he was in a better position to get Susan's cooperation in solving it.

Two-way communication

To get the ball rolling, John brought up the memo incident—asking Susan to describe what happened and why she responded as she did. He avoided making any accusations, which might have short-circuited constructive discussion. As Harry Levinson pointed out in a *Harvard Business Review* article, for communication to be effective, "each party must have a sense of modifying the other." This is doubly true in such problem-solving meetings. John had to be willing to change his views as Susan offered information about her attitude; Susan had to be willing to change hers as John offered information about his side of the story.

Both John and Susan came away from their discussions with a

greater understanding of the factors that influence their working relationship. He discovered that Susan didn't really object to handling rush assignments. Rather, she objected to implications in John's manner that he took her cooperation for granted, that he didn't consider her services important, that he didn't take her seriously. Such human-relations difficulties usually lie at the heart of communication problems.

Private interviews are the best way to resolve them because the privacy gives both parties a chance to speak frankly and it affords the supervisor an opportunity to learn a great deal about himself and how others react to him.

This is an important point because at least two kinds of messages are transmitted in any communication situation—a factual message and an emotional one. When you communicate with another person, you stimulate a reaction quite aside from any information you may wish to convey. To become an articulate communicator, you must learn what kinds of responses you personally provoke. This learning will pave the way toward improved communication in the department and will go a long way toward solving any communication snags that now exist.

A state of flux

Unfortunately, you will not be able to spend six or eight weeks improving communication and then continue on the same plane happily ever after. Why? Because in human communication, the people involved are always changing. Communication is part of an on-going process that involves change in attitudes, beliefs, and behavior. Communicating with others gives you new experiences, each potentially capable of modifying your outlook. Each time you communicate, both you and the listener walk away a little bit changed by the interaction. Your relationship with subordinates is always changing because you, yourself, are involved in a process of change and because they, too, are involved in a process of change.

The fact that human relations are in a constant state of flux implies a major task for you as the leading communicator in the department: to learn how your subordinates respond to each other and to guide these relationships in a constructive channel. This involves doing some

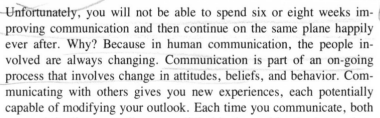

homework on your subordinates. To begin, you might answer the following questions on the basis of your experiences and observations during the past month:

1. In informal chats or formal departmental meetings, which employees tried to reconcile two or more conflicting viewpoints? Cite actual examples. What effect did this have on the employees?

2. Which subordinates have tried to establish procedural rules for attacking problems? Cite actual examples. What effect did this have on other subordinates?

3. Which subordinates have tried to draw out shyer members of the department? How do they go about this? How did the shy employees behave after this? Cite actual examples.

4. Which subordinates make it a habit to speak with a great many people in the department? How does this affect other subordinates individually, their relationships with each other, and their relationship with extroverted subordinates?

5. Which surbordinates aggressively attempt to get their views accepted—by you and by others in the department? Cite actual examples. What effect does this seem to have on the department?

6. Which subordinates have exhibited annoyance with the ideas of other people? Cite actual examples. What effect did this have on those whose ideas were received in this manner?

The answers to these questions should reveal some of the forces that shape human relations in your department. This information can help you iron out difficulties between people so that they can work together more productively. By exerting your own personality, by altering the status of various individuals, and—most important—by stating outright your goals for the department and the quality of cooperation you expect, you can guide people into constructive working relationships.

In this effort, your perceptiveness is all important. You must gain insight into your effect on subordinates and their effect on each other, for it is through behavior that people exchange information, feelings, and attitudes. A thorough knowledge of human relations is the foundation of effective communication.

(Reprinted from SUPERVISORY MANAGEMENT, June 1971)

Lester B. Cundiff

Communicating with Manufacturing Employees

THERE ARE any number of means of communicating with employees, and the most effective communications programs employ several of these methods. The trick is to get a balanced combination for a given work situation. At the New Castle, Del., packaging plant of Amoco Chemicals Corporation, we use various formal and informal methods familiar to most plant people, including bulletin board notices, memoranda, letters, and personal contact, but we also have three formal techniques not widely used in industry but very valuable in our operation, to both management and employees.

Daily information bulletins

The daily information bulletin (DIB) is a one-page, duplicated sheet which deliberately subordinates style, appearance, and even accuracy to the qualities of timeliness and interest. It's our belief that paying too much attention to style and appearance would limit our ability to provide an interesting, up-to-the-minute newsletter. We want accuracy and try to get it, but we're not ashamed to publish a correction tomor-

Manager of the New Castle, Delaware, plant of the Amoco Chemicals Corporation packaging division.

row if, in our concern for timeliness, we let an error slip in today. As a rule, one page is enough for a daily bulletin. If we really need a second page, we'll use it, but we try not to go to two pages more than four or five times a year. We don't seek deathless prose. One of the important features of our DIB is that its authorship is wide; all employees are encouraged to submit items. We may edit them, but don't always do so. If an employee submits a good idea orally, we'll write it for him. At least four different members of management have at times edited the DIB. Usually, the editor is the plant manager, the manufacturing superintendent, or the head of the finishing department, but this division of labor wasn't planned—it just happened.

We have a folder of backlogged items ready to go, so we can always fill our one page with little effort. The backlogged items are the "feature stories" of our bulletin. They include paragraphs on safety, fringe benefits, personalities, product information, and customer information. We try to run them in small series, like our recent "13 Things You Should Know About Lead-Free Gasoline," which, with the preface, took 14 days.

The real meat and potatoes of the DIB are the daily production figures. We agonized a long time about whether to publish these in the weekly bulletin we had before November 1968, but we had no hesitation about publishing them in a "Daily Strike Bulletin" put out for salaried personnel who were operating the plant during a 1968 strike. We found the daily production figures to be such strong motivators that we decided when the strike was over we'd change the weekly bulletin to a daily, and publish the production figures.

The daily production figures are the first two items every day. Item one is always the daily totals, broken down by shift to stimulate a mild competition. Item two is always a list of outstanding performances by individual slitter-packer teams. (This is the only place in the plant where individual performance can be accurately measured.) Item two in particular, and to a lesser extent item one, tell us the DIB is being read. The slitters and packers know their daily production; when we fail to recognize an outstanding performance in the DIB, we hear about it promptly (and write a special, longer note the next day). The effectiveness of this reporting is indicated by the fact that slitting department production per slitter man-hour in the 18th month of the DIB showed an increase of 45 percent.

Besides the daily production figures, to be interesting and/or useful, other items that require timeliness are personals, such as announcements of births, deaths, marriages, for-sale, five-year pins, new hires, military leaves, and promotions. But the DIB is also an official publication, required reading for all employees. It spots minor rule changes, restatement and clarifications of rules, and reminders when rules begin to be ignored, and it also alerts employees when a new procedure has been published or an old one reissued. The DIB is signed by the plant manager to emphasize its official status.

The typist who issues the DIB every day works from a sheaf of items handed her by the editor of the day, usually numbered in the order they should appear. She types the stencil, reads the copy, and has it signed, then duplicates and distributes it. Copies go to a list of management personnel through the company mail, and enough copies are put in racks in the plant to supply those who want to take one. (Sometimes we even remember to mail a copy to someone who is out sick or on vacation.)

Management "advisories"

The management advisory (MA) is a weekly bulletin for supervisory and management personnel. A note at the top cautions that it is "not to be circulated except to official distribution," but the material published is rarely confidential; when confidential material is published, this fact is noted at the beginning of the item. The MA was initiated to keep supervisory personnel better informed than the rank and file. This is hard to do, since the DIB tells all employees almost everything, but the MA does it by publishing:

- Advance notice of new developments, when possible.
- More detail than the DIB—for example, the amount of an appropriation for new equipment.
- Points of specific interest to supervisors, such as current grievances, grievance answers, contract interpretations, and arbitration awards.
- Guidance about handling unusual situations, such as a drunk man in the plant or a fight between employees.
- Comments about costs, profits, and other hard financial facts as far as they can be released to the foreman level.

The MA runs from one to three pages and averages about two and a half pages a week. It is typed on Thursday afternoon or Friday morning from a sheaf of notes collected during the week; a duplicated copy is mailed to the home address of each member of management except those in the front office, to minimize the risk of strayed copies. Because the MA is considered valuable for reference, the copies are punched, and each recipient has a three-ring binder for them. Occasionally, items refer to previous mentions, to emphasize this reference value.

Feedback meetings

All employees seem to appreciate the opportunity to be heard by their superior, but only a few appear to be willing to write down their complaints and/or comments for the suggestion box, and even fewer are uninhibited enough to seek out a superior and make an unsolicited face-to-face comment. We have found that a series of feedback meetings helps to fill this gap. These meetings are substituted for the hour that is usually devoted to safety meetings and are held every six or eight months. The plant manager presides in a very informal way, usually seated on a table, with his principal staff members present and taking notes, for a group of about 25 employees and their direct supervisors.

The plant manager usually begins with a five- or ten-minute monologue on topics he believes will be of immediate interest, such as business prospects, actions taken on the basis of previous feedback meetings, new products, or organizational developments. A little propaganda may be included, such as emphasis on the need for greater productivity, "buy your safety shoes now," "contribute to the United Fund," and other comments on current campaigns.

The rest of the time is devoted to hearing the employees. To get things started, it may be necessary to ask provocative questions: "Are you satisfied with the slitter yield you're getting on B shift?" "Can you increase it?" "How?" In most cases a little of this will be enough to get the comments (mostly critical) flowing freely. We don't at the time provide formal answers to the questions raised in most cases; we do, however, study every comment and take appropriate actions, and a note in the DIB is sometimes published to announce the action taken.

Probably, we'll never be able to communicate well enough with our employees, but the three methods described here have proved to be pluses in our plant. Although one stemmed from a strike situation, I suggest that the time to start them is in a calmer atmosphere, not during an organizing drive or a strike, or in other circumstances that strain relations, when you may be suspected of ulterior motives. Lines of employee communications should be opened when it's easy to do, but in any case, events should not be allowed to close those lines.

(Reprinted from PERSONNEL, September-October 1971)

Roderick Wilkinson

How to Say "It's *your* problem"

IT HAS ALWAYS AMAZED ME that many otherwise efficient managers treat their subordinates the way master sergeants treat their recruits. These supervisors forget that they must do more than give orders if their subordinates are to grow and become more effective in their jobs. They also forget that the kind of approach they take in everyday conversations can vastly influence the motivation and performance of their subordinates. Here is a conversation typical of the kind I've often heard in which a manager tells his subordinate about a job he wants done:

"Harry, I've been concerned about that inventory we're running on the gear line."

"Oh?"

"Dig out the figures and let me see them."

"Why? Are you going to cut the inventory?"

"Maybe. I'll decide that later."

"Okay. I'll get the figures. Will you let me know what you decide?"

"Yes, I will."

This supervisor should have led the conversation so that Harry felt

Employee Relations Manager of a large engineering plant outside Glasgow, Scotland.

that a large part of the responsibility for maintaining acceptable inventory standards belonged to him. For example:

"Harry, is your gear line inventory on standard?"

"Right on the mark."

"You're getting too good! Maybe you should be thinking about a new norm."

"Why? What's wrong with the present one?"

"Nothing—unless you can find a way of having it make us more money by a quicker turnaround. Do you think you can?"

"I'll try. Let me think about it."

In the first conversation, the boss says *"I've* been concerned" about the inventory that *"we're* running" and "let *me* see" the inventory figures so that *"I* can decide" how to cut them. In the second conversation, he spoke about *"your* gear line inventory" which *"you* should be thinking about" until *"you* find a way" to improve it. By using the pronoun "you" instead of "I," this manager has not only done his own job well, but also is encouraging his subordinate to assume responsibility for the gear line inventory and its related costs. He is helping his subordinate to grow.

The same approach is often appropriate when a subordinate comes to his chief with a problem. About 10 years ago, I was assigned to head a department on a day's notice. I was totally unfamiliar with the ins and outs of the job and hardly knew the employees under me or what they did. After I'd been in my new office for two hours, a man walked in and said:

"You probably don't know me. I'm Alex Campbell, the plant safety officer, and I'd appreciate some of your time right away. I've got a tough problem that needs solving now."

He struck me as an intelligent, ambitious man. The more I heard, the more convinced I became that I couldn't help with his specific problem; frankly, I knew as much about factory safety conditions as I knew about bird-watching. I could only listen, absorb what he was saying, and ask some pertinent questions. Yet it was clear that he was discussing a safety problem and he was the safety officer.

When he finished, I said, "Alex, do you know what I would do if I were you?"

His face brightened expectantly. "What?"

"I'd go to the one man in this plant who has the direct responsibility for solving safety problems."

He looked puzzled. "Who's that?"

I said nothing. In two seconds, he got the message.

I have always found that the truly expert manager can create a climate in which his subordinates *want* to assume responsibility and further their personal development. To do this, however, he must do more than set an example. He must plan conversations with subordinates as carefully as he plans any other department operation. I've set up the following checklist for myself:

1. What am I about to say to the employee? Am I requesting information, correcting him, or praising him for a job well-done?

2. How can I get him to think about a problem himself rather than deposit it in my lap?

3. How can I get him to accept responsibility for what we decide and even to take pride in doing so?

The communication traps into which a manager can fall are numerous. The urgency of a situation can elicit terse, clipped directions from a manager which do nothing to encourage the subordinate's self-development. Consider this harassed boss's approach:

"Harry, what about those sprockets?"

"What about them?"

"Well, are they dispatched?"

"Tomorrow."

Rapid-fire action and reaction. The boss may feel efficient, but Harry feels the boss doesn't trust him with a thing. Tomorrow it will be manifolds, the next day, condenser tubes. Expressed anxiety in a boss is like a virus; everybody catches it.

What should be the exchange between the boss and Harry about the sprockets? If the standards of performance were previously agreed on, if Harry is the right man for the job, then the boss should leave Harry alone and hold him accountable for total, measurable results according to their predetermined plan. Given these basic elements, the conversation should go this way:

"Harry, how do you feel about your sprockets dispatch plan?"

"All right. Seems to be working all right."

"Can you think of some way you might improve it?"

"Well, yes. I was thinking about container bulk loading."

"That sounds interesting. Do you know much about it?"

"Not much yet. But I'm going to study the idea at one of the depots next week and work out costs."

"Fine. I'll be interested to hear how you get along."

Any supervisor worth his salt will help foster greater communication with his subordinate by keeping the subordinate's viewpoint in mind when they discuss business matters. For example, the subordinate may be thinking:

1. If you want to criticize me for an error, do it frankly and honestly. Then listen to my side of the story.

2. Can you help me with a problem? I'm not asking you to accept responsibility for things I'm accountable for. What I do need is your advice or your suggestions and, most importantly, your support on what we agree on.

3. Trust me to execute all my responsibilities. If you're judging me, do it by measuring the total results at the end of an agreed period, rather than hounding me about minor details.

(Reprinted from SUPERVISORY MANAGEMENT, July 1969)

William R. Woodruff

Are You in Communication with Your Subordinates?

How WOULD YOU IMPROVE the quality of a message you send out?

- Concentrate on the content to make sure that it is accurate, logical, and clear?
- Concentrate on using the proper words to make your meaning more precise?
- Concentrate on the viewpoint to appeal to the listener's frame of reference?

As good as these measures are, they are of little help in getting through to an employee who is simply not interested in receiving your message. The limitation of these techniques is that they focus primarily on one-way communication.

You can see the limitations of one-way communication in a game that you can try for yourself with a group of friends. Give each participant two copies of a map, and select one city on the map as a starting point. Then read the following aloud: "I am going to give you five instructions to proceed to another location. I will read each instruction slowly and clearly two times. You are to draw your route on the map.

Staff Assistant to the Manufacturing Superintendent, Martinsville, Virginia, Plant, Nylon Manufacturing Division, Textile Fibers Department, E. I. du Pont de Nemours & Co., Inc.

After I start the instructions, you may not ask questions—but are there any questions now?"

I've conducted the game using a map of Ohio. These were my instructions:

1. Start from Chillicothe and proceed north until you come to Route 22.
2. Turn left and, in about a mile, turn right.
3. At the third crossroad turn right.
4. Proceed to the next city (each name circled on the map was, by definition, a city), ignoring all the towns that are in between.
5. Take the first left and proceed to the next city.

After everyone had written down his destination, we began part 2 of the game. We used the same map but revised the rules so that participants could ask questions after each instruction. All questions had to be answered before the next instruction was given.

As you've probably predicted, the second trial showed a dramatic improvement in understanding. Some people, of course, still got lost—but this was the exception rather than the rule.

How to handle feedback

Two-way communication has other advantages over one-way communication. Supervisors have learned that by paying attention not only to what they themselves say but also to employee reactions, they can achieve better understanding. Facial expressions or indications of bodily tension, for example, provide important clues to what is happening to the meaning of your message *in the mind of the recipient*. The problem, of course, is that some people still get "lost."

Feedback improves communication, but the effectiveness of oral communication depends also on how you handle feedback. A supervisor's response to feedback is, in turn, related to his basic assumptions about people. Some bosses assume that employees are stupid and lazy—that they don't want to become involved. These assumptions describe Douglas McGregor's Theory X—the idea that employees must be prodded into working. How does a Theory X boss treat feedback? If he senses that an employee either doesn't understand or doesn't agree with him, he may talk more slowly or more loudly, use shorter and simpler words, or simply repeat his original statements.

TEST YOUR COMMUNICATION QUOTIENT

DO YOU COMMUNICATE WELL? To find out, says Robert Minter of the State University of New York at Buffalo, determine whether you have made any of the following assumptions about communication:

• *That words contain meaning.* Words do not "contain" anything; they are simply acoustical signals that travel via sound waves to someone who may or may not interpret them as you intended. One solution: Be listener-centered, not word-centered. Don't be the communicator who says, "I don't know why they did it wrong—I gave them 'specific' instructions on how to do the job."

• *That the other person is listening.* Although they pride themselves in being good listeners, most people are just 40 to 50 percent attentive. Work-related and nonwork-related problems that preoccupy someone may be beyond his control, so don't depend on his full concentration.

• *That what you say is understood.* There are more ways to interpret a message than there are ways you can think of to express it—a common cause of misunderstandings. The subordinate who doesn't grasp what you say may try to hide the fact. The moral: Don't take understanding for granted.

• *That behavior mirrors attitudes.* Many supervisors cut discussion short when they think that the employee will say or do the right thing. It's an easy trap to fall into—yet research suggests that there is little correspondence between what a person says he thinks and what he actually does. Don't assume that you know a person's attitude because you've been able to predict his behavior—or vice versa.

• *That you have all the facts.* About 30 percent of a message is lost or distorted after having passed through the first two people or levels in a communication chain. One distortion factor: Bad news usually flows downward and good news, upward. Before giving you a message, an employee may filter out information that would place him in a bad light. The higher you climb in an organization, the greater your need to verify the "facts."

—Personnel Journal

Clearly, his communication goal is to get the employee to agree with his opinions, ideas, facts, or information. The pressure he imposes builds up employee resistance, which the boss then interprets as proof of his assumptions about the employee. The phenomenon is called the *self-fulfilling prophecy.*

To the extent that a supervisor conveys his own attitudes, we can say that he has communicated with employees. But there is a vast difference between communicating with and being *in communication with* employees. Being in communication with an employee means that the boss is prepared to be influenced by information, ideas, or attitudes that the employee may have—and vice versa. If, on the other hand, the boss is not receptive, employees will continue to resist him.

Four-way communication

Probably the ideal situation exists when there is four-way communication:

1. The sender transmits a message.
2. The receiver understands the message.
3. The message influences the receiver.
4. The receiver influences the sender.

Here, too, the supervisor's attitude toward subordinates plays a crucial role. If he believes that people want to work, that they are growing, that they want to become involved (these describe McGregor's Theory Y), then the supervisor is operating in a different atmosphere and can expect more favorable results. This self-fulfilling prophecy works to his advantage.

If a subordinate gives a response that causes the boss to change what he says or thinks, a four-way line of communication exists. If, in addition, the boss continues to check the subordinate for secondary feedback to make additional adjustments, the probability increases that there will be mutual and satisfying understanding.

Supervisors who work this way believe that the goal of communication is for the employee to freely express his thoughts, that communication is facilitated when people are willing to express and accept differences in perception. Indirectly, this kind of supervisor is telling employees that he considers them to be valuable people with ideas that deserve the same respect that his do. If he also indicates that he is interested in helping subordinates meet their needs and realize their full potential, his rapport with them will be even stronger.

The rapport creates a climate in which the supervisor receives from employees—on a voluntary basis—information he needs to carry out his daily tasks. This is extremely important because there are times when you are not aware of your ignorance in a particular area.

This free-flowing information is a good measure of the communication climate in your department. If you get helpful information and answers to questions you have not asked or perhaps not even thought of, chances are good that you are *in communication with* your people.

(Reprinted from SUPERVISORY MANAGEMENT, July 1971)

W. S. Hall

Lessons from a Communication Blunder

THERE ISN'T ANY PART of your job that doesn't involve people. They do the work, so your relationship with employees, your communication with them, is all important. It is important on an individual basis and on a group basis as well. If the line of communication between you and just one other employee becomes strained, its weakness may subtract from the loyalty and cooperation of others in the group. Job conditions change; so do people. Hence, lines of communication need constant attention.

This is especially true when a manager is forced to take disciplinary action with an employee. Some of the questions he should consider are:

- What effect will this action have on the individual employee?
- What effect will it have on his co-workers in terms of morale and group efficiency?
- Would another course of action be more advantageous?

The following case study illustrates some of the problems involved in a disciplinary action:

A foreman found that one of his men, Joe, was punching in late almost every Monday morning. He talked with Joe about this and Joe

Manager of Training, Empire-Detroit Steel Division, Cyclops Corporation

readily admitted that he was having trouble getting up on Mondays because of too much celebrating on weekends.

The next Monday, Joe rang in late again and, when the foreman saw him, Joe just grinned. Again, the foreman talked to Joe and asked him to cooperate by getting to work on time. Joe promised that he would try.

However, the following Monday, Joe was late again. This time, the foreman called Joe in and gave him a written reprimand. He also told him that if he was late again, it would mean time off without pay. Joe realized that the foreman meant business and promised that it would not happen again.

For three Mondays in a row, Joe was on time. The foreman began to think that he had solved the problem. But, on the fourth Monday, Joe did not appear. The later it got, the angrier the foreman got.

When Joe finally walked in, the foreman met him at the door. "All right," he said angrily, "you've asked for it. That will cost you time off without pay."

When Joe tried to talk, the foreman shut him off by saying, "I don't want to hear any alibis. You can't talk me into changing my mind."

How would you judge the foreman's action? Appropriate? Inappropriate? Perhaps this additional information will help you make up your mind.

During the remainder of that day and the next, the foreman noticed that the other men were acting cold and resentful toward him. He couldn't figure it out until another foreman told him that the man he had suspended was late, not because he had been on a bender the night before, but because he had wrecked his car on the way to work to keep from hitting a boy on a bike who had swerved in front of him. Joe had even refused to go to a doctor to check for possible injury to himself because he wanted to get to work as soon as possible.

These additional facts obviously change the complexion of this case. They also point up the necessity of not jumping to conclusions and of getting the whole story.

In gathering facts, it's important to:

Review the record: This includes all you know about the employee, not just information contained in his file.

Talk with people concerned: Joe's foreman didn't do this. Yet he

COMMUNICATION PROBLEM—SOLVED OR UNSOLVED?

There's only one way to find out if you've really solved a communication problem, and that is to check the results of the action you have taken.

- *What indicators should you look for?* Watch for changes in output, attitudes, and relationships. Find out how your corrective action has affected the group as well as the person with whom you had the specific problem.
- *How soon should you follow up?* It's a matter of judgment. But you can usually make your first check as soon as you can reasonably expect results.
- *How often should you check?* This, too, is a matter of judgment. Sometimes you must keep tabs on a situation for quite a while to be sure that the problem has cleared up and that your action hasn't created other problems.

---

could have gotten crucial information from the men who knew about the accident.

Get opinions and feelings: Right or wrong, what a person thinks or feels is real to him.

Find out what company rules apply: This includes both written and unwritten rules.

After systematically gathering all relevant facts, the next step is to weigh the information. We've all seen people behave abnormally and thought we knew the reason for such behavior. But there's no guarantee that your point of view explains the story fully. If you want to understand people, it helps to try to see things from their point of view. Do the facts that you have gathered fit together? Can you find gaps or contradictions? Joe's foreman made a pattern of facts with only partial information. He ignored Joe's recent "on time" record and decided that Joe had been on another bender. Furthermore, he took action without first considering alternative actions and without considering the effect that his action with Joe would have on the rest of the work group. Sometimes a supervisor has to make a communication blunder in order to realize how important human relations are to him.

It's better still, of course, to avoid problems before they start. Here are some things you can do every day to keep communication lines strong and to discover any sore points that may exist.

1. *Let each worker know how he is getting along.* A supervisor must determine what to expect from each employee and then tell him what it is. Every employee should know how he is getting along.

2. *Give credit when credit is due.* Notice that little word *when*. Timing is important. Suppose you do something "extra" and expect your boss to pat you on the back. Instead, he doesn't say a word and forgets about it for a couple of weeks. When he finally does say something, you will be pleased. But in the meantime you probably will not have done anything else extra because you didn't get credit the first time.

3. *Tell people in advance about changes that will affect them.* And don't forget to tell them why the changes are necessary. It's human nature for a person to resist and resent changes that he's had no part in bringing about. But if people are told about change in advance and told why the change is being made, they are more likely to cooperate.

4. *Make the best use of each employee's ability.* Never look upon a crew or a work group as consisting of people with similar abilities—even though all may be holding the same job. By getting to know your subordinates, you'll find that each has a slightly different repertoire of skills as well as a different level of expertise. Assigning new tasks to the right people will enable you to make the most efficient use of manpower and to contribute to the employee's development as well.

These four actions are the foundation of good human relations. They aren't new—but they aren't just theoretical, either. They really work.

This is not to say that they will prevent personnel problems from arising. Many factors affect employees, and any one of them can create trouble on the job. If, for example, an employee has been up all night because of illness in the family, both his production and his disposition are likely to suffer. The work a person does may affect him: One man will like his job; another will hate it. Some people take pride in doing good work; others do just enough to get by. A person's background and education will affect his outlook. These and other factors make people different from one another. The important message for supervisors is this: If you want to get your people to do what you want done, when it should be done, the way you want it done, and—most important—because they want to do it, you must treat them as individuals. The more you know about what motivates your subordinates and why they behave as they do, the better chance you have of doing a good job.

This doesn't mean that you have to spend most of your time worrying about how to treat people. But you must be sensitive to changes. There has to be a reason if a man who is always cheerful suddenly gets sullen or surly, a man who usually turns out a lot of work starts loafing, or a man with an excellent attendance record suddenly becomes an absentee problem. When behavior is abnormal, you should know that the employee has a problem and find out if it is anything on which you should take action.

The author gives special acknowledgment to Henry McClelland, Training Director, Goodyear Atomic Corporation, for his assistance in developing the material for this article.

(Reprinted from SUPERVISORY MANAGEMENT, December 1971)

J. R. Cranwell

The Fine Art of Listening

How is your listening i.q.? If you think it's high, just listen to Dr. Ralph Nichols, a leading authority on the art of listening. According to him, studies have shown that college freshmen retain only 50 per cent of a 10-minute lecture and lose half of this material in 48 hours. And listening efficiency is just as low among churchgoers hearing a sermon, jurors receiving instructions from a judge, and business managers hearing a message from a superior.

Dr. Nichols has described nine ways in which people can become better listeners:

1. *Find the speaker's subject useful.* When the topic of the talk is announced, the poor listener may call the subject dull or old hat (and perhaps it is), so he goes off on a mental tangent. The good listener may be just as unimpressed with the topic. But being trapped in the audience, he tunes in on the speaker for any new knowledge he can use later. The good listener sifts the wheat from the chaff.

2. *Concentrate on the talk, not the delivery.* A poor listener may find fault with the speaker's delivery and go off on a tangent because the speaker is so stupid. The good listener may start at the same point, but he reaches a different conclusion. He realizes the speaker knows a lot more about the subject than he does and makes every effort to pick his brains.

3. *Withhold evaluation until comprehension is complete.* A poor listener becomes overstimulated and almost immediately begins framing questions or rebuttals for the speaker. The good listener hears the man out before judging his statements.

4. *Try to get the major ideas of the subject.* A poor listener may say, "I listen only for facts." He retains a few facts but garbles many and loses most of them. The good listener concentrates on the concepts the speaker is trying to develop. He understands the central ideas and uses them as links to tie together the whole talk, with the supporting facts attached to these links.

5. *Adjust note taking to the pattern of the speaker.* A poor listener attempts to outline on paper everything he hears. To him an outline and notes are the same thing. But two months later he is hopelessly confused when he tries to figure out the notebook. The good listener is flexible. How or if he takes notes depends on the organizational pattern the speaker uses. One recommended way for taking notes is listing facts and principles of the talks separately.

6. *Be attentive.* A poor listener fakes attention to the speaker while his mind wanders all over the place. A good listener is not relaxed or passive. He works hard to absorb the subject.

7. *Tackle difficult material.* A poor listener habitually evades intellectual or thought-exercising subjects and when confronted with a tough topic isn't conditioned to absorb much of anything. A good listener develops an interest in important, challenging matters and grasps the meaning of what is said.

8. *Don't be blocked by emotion-laden words.* Some words will create a barrier between speaker and audience. Dr. Nichols, for example, once used the word *evolution* in a talk to college freshmen and later discovered that 40 per cent of the audience had tuned him out, for they associated evolution with atheism. A good listener, however, does not let one word or several stand between him and the substance of the message.

9. *Profit from the differential between speech speed and thought speed.* An audience generally thinks at the rate of 400 words a minute, or four times faster than the speaker talks. A poor listener wastes this time differential by drifting back and forth between the speaker and his own thoughts. Dr. Nichols recommends three ways a good listener can gain from this time gap. First, anticipate the speaker's next point. If you guess right, that point comes to your mind twice; if you guess wrong, you immediately compare your guess with the point he does make and learn by contrast and comparison. Second, identify what the speaker uses for supporting evidence. And third, periodically recapitulate the speaker's remarks; this will double your ability to understand and retain their content.

In stressing the importance of good listening, Dr. Nichols referred to a study made by Loyola University on the question: "What is the most important single attribute of an effective manager?"

The study showed that listening to the individual employee is the most effective way for a manager to know and accurately size up the personalities of the people in his department. The most common report received from thousands of men who testified that they like their supervisors ran this way:

"I like my boss. He listens to me. I can talk to him."

(Reprinted from SUPERVISORY MANAGEMENT, September 1969)

Philip Anthony
William P. Anthony, Ph.D.

Now Hear This:
Some Techniques of Listening

IT's COMMON KNOWLEDGE that a good supervisor is a good listener. After all, listening is an important part of effective communication between managers and subordinates at all levels in an organization. And the supervisor who makes a point of listening is making conscious use of an important tool in his day-to-day dealings with others.

Effective communication does not occur automatically. In fact, the communication process is often depicted by means of six steps: ideation, encoding, transmission, reception, decoding, and action. *Ideation* is simply the conception of a thought or idea. *Encoding* is symbolizing the idea either orally, by written word, or by electrical or magnetic impulse. *Transmission* is the movement of the symbols from sender to receiver. *Reception* occurs when the symbols are received by the listener. *Decoding* involves the listener's interpretation of the symbols received. *Action* is some behavior or activity that is induced by the received message. Sometimes this means simply storing or remembering the information.

Supervisors must be aware of blockages and distortions that occur

Department of Personnel Administration, Owens-Illinois, Inc.
Assistant Professor of Management, The Florida State University

throughout the whole communication process. Let's see how to reduce these blockages and distortions at the listening end of communication.

Empathy in communication

The boundaries for understanding expand when empathy exists. In fact, the key to effective listening is empathy—the ability to see an idea or concept from another's viewpoint. You must be aware of another's background, values, and attitudes when you listen to what he is saying. Simply put, it means putting yourself in another person's shoes. When you practice empathy, you listen nonevaluatively. You listen without arguing or passing judgment on what is being said at the time. You listen to gain an understanding of how the problem looks to the speaker in view of his information sources, goals, background, and attitudes. Under these positive conditions, the speaker's defense mechanisms usually relax, since he no longer finds it necessary to argue with his listener.

Empathy versus agreement

Keep in mind that empathy is understanding and doesn't necessarily involve *agreement*. Try to recognize that people are often afraid to try to understand what is being said because they are afraid that they might agree with it. If a newly agreed-with piece of information conflicts with your attitudes and beliefs, a condition can arise within you known as *cognitive dissonance*. Cognitive dissonance is a system of nonfitting attitudes or beliefs that brings about internal psychological conflict. In trying to avoid this condition, you as a listener might refuse to try to understand information that is in conflict with what you already believe. In this case, you must have enough confidence in the logical consistency and validity of your own beliefs and attitudes so that you can relax any defensiveness and try to understand new information. You should realize that you do not necessarily have to agree with the information just because you understand it.

If the speaker interprets empathy and understanding as agreement by the listener when agreement is not intended, the listener can make his position clear by giving whatever explanation is necessary. Remember, you can disagree without being disagreeable. You might say, for example, when the listening process is completed, "John, I understand what you are saying and you have some very good points—but I don't agree with them. Here are my reasons.''

Advantages of effective listening

Among the pluses for effective listening is that it fosters beneficial interpersonal relationships. It indicates a willingness to understand another person. This implies a respect for the other person. And this respect maintains and builds the other person's ego and own sense of self-respect and dignity. It also often results in a reciprocal feeling of respect between two people. Let's look at several situations in which maintaining beneficial interpersonal relationships through effective listening is especially important.

Problem identification

Identifying problems is a difficult task because supervisors are often aware of a problem only through its symptoms. Symptoms are clues to or manifestations of more basic problems that usually are hidden. Through effective listening, various symptoms may be dealt with to uncover the basic problem.

To identify the problem, repeat what a person says. Express it in your own words. Reflecting feeling is a valuable technique for identifying problems. For example, you might say, ''John, you feel that because you are the senior employee, you should have been assigned to that new machine. Is that correct?'' The point is that the words used are not as important as the attitude reflected. Genuine interest in what the other person is saying is a necessity and must be conveyed in a casual, conversational way.

Naturally, this technique can be overdone. Excessive repetition may indicate to the speaker that the listener is not paying close attention or that he is mocking him. To be effective, the technique must be practiced consistently.

Grievances

Establish a definite time to listen to grievances. Then, devote your undivided attention to listening to the grievance or complaint. Avoid glancing at papers on the desk or allowing excessive interruption from phone calls or messages. Make sure that the grieving employee feels that you are interested in listening to his grievance. And remember, what may have been a simple question may prove to be the beginning of a serious grievance.

Keep in mind that if you don't listen to the employee who is a union member you may have more, far-reaching problems later. Such an employee might take his grievance to the union steward, who is usually a sympathetic listener. The end result might then become an arbitration case.

Progress interviews

A supervisor should spend at least 50 percent of a progress interview listening. The key is in the type of question you should ask. For example, you might try one of the following kinds of questions. Each is effective.

- "John, the waste goal we agreed on was no more than 2 percent. It has been running 4 percent. What must we do to bring this under control?"
- "What plans do you have to improve your ability to read blueprints?"
- "What is it you enjoy most about your work?"
- "What phase of your work do you find most difficult?"
- "What do you consider the most important part of your job?"
- "How can we improve the operation?"

Remember to follow other basic tenets of performance appraisal carefully. The tenets include mutually determined goals that are specific and measurable. Tabulate the results of the interview so that the performance can be measured against goals and can be compared with the performance of others.

Performance improvement

The organizational goal requires specific types of employee effort. It matters little whether it's a specific level of probability, a desired quality level, the delivery of a specified service, or the maximum in production efficiency. When these goals are not being reached, it is because employee efforts are not what they should be. You must identify which employees have not performed adequately and why, so that the performance can be corrected. Consider whether the employee knows specific organizational goals. Does he know how his departmental and individual goals are integrated with corporate goals? Is he committed to these goals? Does he know what is required of him in his job? And does he have adequate training, so that he can perform his job properly?

Phrase your questions so that the employee will explain why he's doing what he is. For example, you might say, "John, look at this printing. We can't ship something like this. Let's get it corrected." But this might be better phrased: "John, look at this printing. Do you think we should ship something like this? What seems to be the problem? Perhaps we should briefly review how you are running the job."

Group meetings

In conducting employee group meetings, a supervisor should spend a majority of the time listening to suggestions from the group. He should moderate the meeting and should guide the discussion, but he should also encourage the employees present to participate. He should be receptive to their comments and attempt to understand them. Try, for example, asking:

- "Here's the problem we are having on waste. (Then explain the problem.) What can be done about it?"
- "What can we do to reduce accidents?"
- "How can we improve quality?"
- "How can we implement the introduction of this process to cause minimum disruption?"

New ideas

An extremely difficult yet important time to practice effective listening is when one is presented with a new idea. Here, the intended message can be distorted by the listener because of cognitive dissonance, discussed previously. This happens in several ways. Studies show that people listen selectively. They interpret what they hear in light of their own attitudes and beliefs. They tend to eliminate what does not fit, to make it fully conform to their preconceptions. This process is called selective perception. Everyone practices it to some extent when they listen to new ideas.

If the listener finds that he consistently disagrees with the ideas, he might reject the validity and truthfulness of the source and stop listening. He is now practicing selective exposure: that is, listening only to sources that have tended to reinforce his preconceptions.

Beware of selective retention—the final manner in which a new idea is often distorted. Here, a person remembers only what seems to fit his existing structure of attitudes and beliefs. That which does not fit is forgotten. Thus, new ideas are not acted upon because they are quickly forgotten by the listener.

Conscious self-discipline and practice to overcome these obstacles are essential to effective listening. A supervisor should think of ways in which a novel idea might work instead of rejecting the idea immediately. He should understand the idea before he evaluates it, and he should try to avoid such negatives as, "It won't work," or "It's been tried before." The positive approach—"It may have possibilities; tell me more"—might turn an ordinary suggestion into an unexpected treasure.

Listening to a superior

Three difficulties often occur when a subordinate listens to you.

- He might resent interference in an area for which he feels responsible.
- He might welcome the suggestions or commands, but not fully understand them.
- He might fully understand the recommended course of action, but disagree with it.

In the first case, any suggestion you make might be interpreted by the subordinate as a criticism of his present performance or, worse yet, a criticism of himself as a person. Usually, the subordinate can do very little to correct this feeling. Instead, the supervisor must modify his message and his manner of communicating.

In the second case, if the subordinate is in doubt about what he is being asked to do, he should repeat in his own words what he thinks he has been told. For example, he might say, "To make certain that I don't misunderstand, you want me to. . . ." Tell subordinates to ask for more information even if it's a simple question they are in doubt about.

The third situation requires a great deal of tact. An effective superior will give subordinates plenty of opportunity to express their opinions, to facilitate communication and to generate new and better ideas through discussion. Let them tell you about their disagreement and give you specific reasons for it.

Dealing with the angry person

When you're dealing with someone who is angry, be sure to listen before you talk. Let the person talk and try to understand him. Before you respond to him, give sufficient thought to what he said. Many people wrongly believe that hesitation and reflection are signs of weakness. They take great pride in telling people off, especially in an emotional and angry situation. This usually leads to further angry exchanges and frustrations, which often become manifest in other forms of behavior.

Your reply depends on the nature of his complaint. But you could say, for example, "This thing really has you upset," and take it from there. Or you could say, "You feel that you've been mistreated." Or, "You feel that you shouldn't do it because it's not part of your job." In any case, encourage him to talk it out. Statements such as, "Don't make a fool of yourself," or "You shouldn't talk like that," only add fuel to the fire. If he is angry with you, say, "You feel I have been unfair," or "You feel I'm being unreasonable," depending on the situation. The important thing is to reflect his feelings and give him an opportunity to talk. You gain control when you use this method properly.

(Reprinted from SUPERVISORY MANAGEMENT, March 1972)

DATE